Paperback reprint of the Texana classic

Famous
Texas Feuds

C.L. Douglas

Foreword by Paul H. Carlson

State House
Press

McMurry University
Abilene, Texas

Library of Congress Cataloging-in-Publication Data

Douglas, C.L. (Claude Leroy), 1901-
    Famous Texas feuds / C.L. Douglas.
      p.   cm.
    Reprint. Originally published: Dallas, Tex.: Turner Co., 1936.
    Includes index (1988) and foreword (2007).
    ISBN-13: 978-1-933337-11-1 (pbk. : alk. paper)
    ISBN-10: 1-933337-11-7 (pbk. : alk. paper)
    1. Vendetta--Texas--History--19th century. 2. Texas--History--1846-1950.
    I. Title

F391.D72 1988
976.4'06--dc19

FOREWORD

Gunfighters, gun-fighting, and family and community feuds have long attracted writers, filmmakers, scholars, and the general reading public. Books on such topics are numerous and many go to second and third printings or second editions. Likewise, journal articles, magazine essays, and book chapters that treat gun fighters, gun fighting, and America's gun culture in general appear often. Indeed, one of the more popular books on the American West is entitled *Gun Fighter Nation*.

Famous Texas Feuds is part of the popular tradition. It is a colorfully written account of some of the most notorious intra-community "affairs of honor" in Texas, a state in many ways built on violence, revolution, and long struggles to wrest the land from American Indians determined to hold it. The book, first published in 1936, has gone through several re-printings. And, moreover, it has been the inspiration for similar works, including such scholarly efforts as *Ten Texas Feuds*, *I'll Die Before I Run*, and *No Duty to Retreat*.

Claude Leroy Douglas (1901-1967), the author of *Famous Texas Feuds*, was born in Oklahoma but lived and worked much of his life in Fort Worth. He served as an associate editor of the *Fort Worth Press*, and he worked for forty years for the Scripps-Howard media giant. In addition, from July 1951 to his death he wrote the "Chuckwagon Charlie" column for *The Cattleman* magazine. He authored at least six books of which *Famous Texas Feuds* was the third. He was among the first persons to write in a serious way about the Texas navy, the Texas Rangers, and the flamboyant Texas governor W. Lee O'Daniel. In recent years, the title of his popular book *Cattle Kings of Texas* (1936) has been borrowed by more than one contemporary author writing about Texas livestock raisers.

In *Famous Texas Feuds* Douglas writes with grace and power. If he is a bit wordy at times, he should be forgiven, for his style is representative of his time and its great stories. Indeed, Douglas is a wonderful storyteller who finds drama and poignancy in even the most deadly contests he describes. But don't get me wrong. The feuds that are the subject of this book resulted in murder, arson, threat and intimidation, and destruction in shocking proportions. In most cases what started as a minor disagreement between two families escalated into community-wide, mob-driven hostilities.

Most people who participated in the feuds regretted being involved. Many tried to stay out, but local pressure and threats of various degrees, including death, forced them into the affairs. While thugs, toughs, and ne'er-do-wells were the major participants, so were large-scale cotton planters and cattlemen with huge herds—people with much to lose. Law abiding farmers got involved, as did preachers, teachers, and women; plus doctors, dentists, shopkeepers, and lawyers.

The deadliest feuds became tragic affairs, dominated by mob violence and what Douglas calls "Mr. Lynch Law." General outlawry and thievery started the first and bloodiest feud in Texas, the Regulator-Moderator (Shelby County) War in the 1840s. In a general sense it pitted during the Republic of Texas era established Texans against newly arrived residents. Some feuds, such as the Mason County War (1875) and the Salt War (1877), were ethnic/racial clashes: the former pitted German-Texans against other American-Texans, and the latter saw Mexicans and Mexican-Americans fighting Anglo-Americans. The Sutton-Taylor Feud in De Witt County began with disputes between neighboring families over cattle. Eventually, scores of people became involved. The Jaybird-Woodpecker feud of 1888 in Fort Bend County grew from political differences related to the Reconstruction Era in Texas, including carpetbagger Republicans and native Texas Democrats and their struggle to gain the votes of the black population in the county.

Sometimes women took important parts. Helen Mar Moorman, for example, assumed a key role in the Shelby County War when she led a "Regulator" charge against a "Moderator" position at Beauchamp Farm. The decisive battle—and the timely arrival of President Sam Houston—was a significant event in bringing the long and bloody feud to an end.

Famous Texas Feuds tells these stories, stories that represent dark and gloomy, but unforgettable, chapters in the long history of the state. They are stories, as Douglas himself writes, of "how peculiar conditions," an errant comment, or an unthinking act in a moment of anger like a match to a dynamite fuse "launched" a whole series of bloody consequences.

Douglas approached his writing of books only after careful and detailed investigation. *Famous Texas Feuds* as a result represents several months of systematic research, including an examination of old documents, newspapers, official records, personal letters, and scrapbooks. In addition, Douglas conducted a number of interviews with participants or their descendents. The exhaustive research combined with the author's lively writing style has produced this exceptional study about some of the most intriguing but unfortunate events in nineteenth century Texas.

Paul H. Carlson
Texas Tech University

CONTENTS

H. CLAY PLEASANTS, the fighting district judge who helped establish
law and order in DeWitt County.

INTRODUCTION

One of the chapters in Texas history—that covering one of its more lurid periods—was written, not with the ink and pen, but with the lead of the Winchester rifle and the slugs of a double-barreled shotgun.

As a result, that particular period, the decade of the 1870s, might well be termed the "bloody years."

It was a decade which found its background of dissension in the program of Reconstruction which followed the War Between the States; its bloody sequences fostered by a spirit of outlawry born of the war, and of the cattle stealing troubles attendant on the closing of the open range.

With the exception of the East Texas conflict between the Regulators and the Moderators in the days of the Republic, most of the greater Texas feuds—which usually were community rather than family affairs—occurred in the '70s.

This book tells that story—how peculiar conditions among a people brought into play the shotguns and rifles of vengeance, and launched a time of tumult.

—C. L. DOUGLAS.

Fort Worth, Texas.

THE REGULATORS AND THE MODERATORS

CHAPTER ONE

PRELUDE TO MURDER

On a mid-summer evening in the year 1837 an assorted company of eight gentlemen, arriving in an obscure village on the west bank of the Sabine, signed their names on the greasy guest-book in a modest hostelry maintained by a portly individual who gloried in the simple monniker of Uncle Ben.

That they were gentlemen of some distinction was plainly evident from the flourish used as they identified themselves upon the ledger—for the party boasted no less than three Colonels, two Majors and two Captains —and Uncle Ben, wise in the ways of the western world, smiled to himself as he watched his guests step up to sign.

Uncle Ben knew the breed—better, perhaps, than any other man in all the Neutral Strip dividing the state of Louisiana and the Texas Republic. As keeper of the only inn for miles about the river crossing he had witnessed for many months the ever-growing influx of these titled adventurers who, drawn by the glamor of the Texas Revolution, had journeyed west in search of gold and glory.

Now when the eighth man came to sign the book Uncle Ben tilted his eyebrows in amazement, for this fellow—a burly but pleasant appearing person whose buckskin pants supported two cap-and-ball pistols at the

1

waistband—entered himself without any appendage whatsoever. The surprised proprietor said nothing, as befit a host in those wild days along the border, but when the supper hour arrived and the company had grouped itself about the board it was noted by the stranger that the most comfortable place had been reserved for him; and that, moreover, Uncle Ben insisted he take the choicest portions of baked fowl and venison steak. This over-attention, at length, became quite embarrassing but the burly guest likewise held his tongue, and wondered.

When morning arrived and the guests came down to settle up their score the puzzle solved itself, for as the colonels, majors and captains inquired the total of their fare Uncle Ben charged each a dollar and a half until he reached the eighth man on the list. Then he paused.

"What is my bill, sir?" asked the stranger, noting the hesitancy.

"Not a cent, sir," replied Uncle Ben, "and if you will stay with me a week it shan't cost you a penny. You are the first private gentleman it has been my good fortune to meet since I left the states, and the pleasure of conversing with you, sir, has been more than sufficient pay."

So saying, he watched the company depart—but not without first wondering which among the officer personnel was the horse thief, which the murderer, and which the bloody bandit. He had his own ideas about the young man who carried no title at all—for, as I have pointed out, old Uncle Ben knew his western world; knew, too, where those military cognomens had been born.

The ferryman on the Sabine was getting rich, comfortably rich. A shrewd and ingenious Yankee, whose continued lease on life is explained by the fact that Yankee had not yet become a fighting word in Texas, this boatman had been quick to sense the current mania for military fame. Accordingly, he had caused to be printed in the states an imposing batch of regimental commissions forged with the signatures of governors all the way from Vermont to Virginia, and done in the accredited fancy whorls of the time.

These he always kept locked in a drawer at his shanty, and upon payment of a stipulated sum the ferryman would bring out whichever honor his customer might prefer—anything from a captaincy to a generalship—fill in the blank space left for the new arrival's name, and thus foist upon the Republic of Texas a brand new son of Mars.

It made not the slightest difference what manner of pedigree might be attached to these roving gentry, too often rogues of the deepest dye. What really mattered to the ferryman was the cash which lined their pockets, and there is no possible way of determining just how many horse thieves and cut-throats he did send on their way rejoicing, and clothed in the respectability a military commission is commonly supposed to carry.

This explains one reason why Texas, as one contemporary described it, was peopled "with more colonels than would be sufficient to officer the combined armies of the world, even were all mankind combined into a

standing army—men who never so much as killed a
snowbird with a gun in all their lives."

But whither did these colonels and majors and captains go after receiving their titular papers and depart-
ing from the precincts of the border? Some, of course,
pushed into central Texas to take whatever employment,
either civil or military, the young Republic might offer.
Many considered they had gained their goal once they
crossed the watery line marking the boundary between
the States and Texas, and these were content to settle
down on the westward side of the Sabine and celebrate
with a continual round of libations a late escape from
the hands of a sheriff or the rope of a posse.

Thus the country opposite Louisiana became rendezvous and refuge for the most villainous collection of
murderers, thieves and swindlers that ever migrated
from one nation to another. It was a piney land particularly suited to the purpose. It was unhampered by the
heavy hand of law, a place where no man need strain
his back with loathsome toil—at least while fat beeves
and hogs remained in the pens of more honest settlers,
and while corn yet grew in the fields. Over across the
line the man who stole his neighbor's stock was called
a thief and became fair game for the sheriff's gun,
while over here the victims feared him for the deed—
and called him major, or captain, or colonel. The ferry
on the Sabine was the difference.

Small wonder that the spirit of lawlessness became
infectious. What with desperadoes settling down in
homes and making no attempt to hide their calling;
what with a total absence of statute books and written

rules of order, it is not at all surprising that the social system of East Texas took on a color all its own. It was a place where "Judge Lynch" sat upon the bench, where the populace took the place of jury, and where a low-limbed pine tree constituted the instrument of chastisement on those occasions when such measures were considered necessary.

In a way, however, this seed of disorder fell on fallow ground, for even the larger portion of the older settlers in the Municipality of the Tenaha—embracing Shelby, Harrison and Panola counties—were men who had departed from other lands under the shadow of deeds they did not care to mention. It went even further than that. As Dr. Levi H. Ashcraft, late of Tyler, points out in a lengthy document he penned in those days:

"The influence of religion was unfelt, and the restraints of civilized society entirely disregarded. Even those who had been pious in the old states could not escape the general infection and many of them soon became as reckless and immoral as those with whom they were compelled to mingle, thus exemplifying the truth of that trite saying that 'man is the creature of circumstance.' The ministers of the gospel themselves, who came out as missionaries, did not escape the contamination; for some of them proved greater adepts in villainy than those from whom they had learned their original lessons, by running in an incredibly short time through the whole catalogue of infamy, and Judas-like betraying their God because he was not bodily present upon the earth."

There you have the picture from the human stand-
point, but there was yet something else—the land itself.

Real estate titles, to put it plainly, were in a mess.
Prior to the Texas Republic, prior even to Mexican
regime, the Spanish crown had made grants along the
eastward shore of the Sabine, and many Americans
had taken up residence there. They still were in that
area in 1819 when the treaty between the United States
and Spain established the river as the boundary line
between their respective territories. They still were
there when the Mexican Republic was formed in 1824,
but shortly thereafter they began moving across the
stream to establish homes on the westward bank.

These settlers, however, had no means of obtaining
titles to these particular holdings until the law of
Texas-Coahuila was passed in 1834. Then ample provisions were made, the government granting a league
of land—some four thousand acres—to heads of families, and one-fourth of a league to single men.

Under the Mexican government there had been civil
law in the region, but in most respects it was extra-
ordinarily peculiar. Administered by a local *alcalde* it
provided, for instance, that in cases of theft the ag-
grieved party should receive from the aggressor, if
apprehended, restitution four-fold in the same kind of
property stolen. In cases of personal violence each
person was expected to look to himself, or his friends,
for justice.

This point has special significance in the light of
events to follow—a point equally significant with the
fact that these early families along the Sabine inter-

married and formed among themselves a sort of fellowship which marked them as a class. They lived in peace,
and then—

Revolt . . . San Jacinto . . . and a new rule over the
section west of the river; and worst of all—the arrival
of the "colonels" and the "captains." The old settlers
had not yet begun to consider seriously what influence
this great influx of new citizens might have on the
social life of the community; they had other worries.
What, under this change in government, would their
newly acquired land titles be worth now? It was not
long until the answer was forthcoming.

The new Republic hurriedly passed a law providing
for the election in each county of a local judge and a
board of land commissioners whose job would be the
issuance of land certificates to those who made the
proper claim. Each claimant was to be required, as he
appeared before the board, to make oath that he was a
citizen of Texas at the time of the Declaration of
Independence, that he did not in any way assist the
enemy, and that he did not absent himself from the
country to avoid service in the army of independence—
all this to be attested by two witnesses.

Texas, of course, had plenty of land and the Republic
practically gave away large tracts to lure new citizens,
but the foregoing provisions pertained only to those
already established—those who held choice acreage.

But when the elections were held the "colonels"
voted, and it soon became apparent to the old-timers
that the newcomers were to hold the whip hand in the
administration of county affairs. Almost immediately

fraudulent land certificates, some even bearing fictitious names, began to flood the country to the extent that it soon became almost impossible to distinguish between the bogus and the genuine. The county land commissioners, some of them past masters in the swindler's art, held the country in their grasp.

Huge tracts changed hands, sometimes for a consideration amounting to little more than the proverbial song. Dealers trafficked in certificates in the full knowledge on both sides that they were not worth the paper on which they were printed. Holders of new certificates, obtained through false swearing and other villainous practices, "sold" property from under the very feet of the old settlers and original homesteaders. Land pirates invaded the country in regiments to swell the hordes of horse thieves and gun slingers already firmly rooted in the population.

Quite unconsciously at first, the people on the west bank of the Sabine began forming into two factions— the Old Settlers against the New. And there was no law—except that which had been handed down from the Mexican *alcaldes,* an unwritten law of eye for eye and tooth for tooth as old as Genesis itself.

Hate swept the Tenaha like a sullen wind—a fitting prelude to murder!

The greatest of the Texas feuds was in the making —the first of those grim episodes which invariably began in some minor incident but which involved, before the end, hundreds of men recruited from the surrounding countrysides. In this lay the difference between the Texas wars and the family affairs of Kentucky, Tennessee and other states beyond the Mississipi.

Another thing—the participants in the war between the Regulators and the Moderators, the first and greatest of the Texas feuds, appear to have based the conflict on a famous working model. There is more than passing evidence that the literature of the Scottish clans was widely read in this far corner of the wild frontier.

It is difficult to conceive a thing such as that which occurred in East Texas during the early 1840's. If the participants in the affair were typical of early Texas fighters small wonder that Santa Anna's Mexicans fled the boundaries of the country . . .

CHAPTER TWO

THE GATHERING OF THE CLANS

Captain Charles W. Jackson, like so many others of his day, came to Texas suddenly—and without so much as an extra pair of pants.

In fact, he arrived so hurriedly that he did not even linger long enough at the Sabine ferry to take unto himself one of the military commissions so much in vogue at the time; but this was not at all necessary in his particular case.

The title which he bore was valid. Mr. Jackson lately had been captain of a river boat which plied the Mississippi and the Red, a lucrative position he would have been loath to relinquish had it not been for circumstances involving the sudden death of one merchant and the wounding of another in the Louisiana town of Alexandria.

After that he had sensed a certain restraint on the part of the townspeople—especially after hearing that a thirty thousand dollar reward had been put on his head, and a small cannon mounted on the wharf to greet him on his next arrival. But even these things had not served to give the captain pause.

He had arranged at once to make Alexandria a port of call, but with two guns mounted upon his boat, a cannon on the hurricane deck and a mortar on the bow. He then dropped anchor off the town and sent a man

10

to announce his arrival and invite the citizens to open fire—if they dared. The anger of the citizens apparently had cooled and the captain, finding no excuse to carry out his threat to burn the town, dropped down to New Orleans, where he successfully dodged a sheriff's posse in that port and then sailed back up the river.

They got him at last in Shreveport, but while being transported by boat to the city which thirsted for his blood he dived overboard one dark and moonless night, swam ashore, stole a horse, and headed westward, a barefoot fugitive from justice.

With this colorful background Captain Charlie Jackson crossed the Sabine during the early days of 1839— little suspecting the major role he was to play in one of the greatest blood and thunder dramas ever enacted within the boundaries of the Texas Republic. He sent for his family and a stock of goods and opened a store in Shelbyville, but it seemed that wherever Charlie went trouble never was far behind.

A tall, sober-faced man with a mouthful of teeth and an unsmiling countenance, he was a stranger in a strange land—but not for long. He had found one former acquaintance when he arrived in town, one Maulheel Johnson, but Maulheel gathered up his belongings and departed . . . he knew Mr. Jackson all too well.

Now it happened that the captain had been in Shelbyville but a short time when there came to his ears news of certain trouble between a Mr. Joe Goodbread and a Mr. Albert George, the current candidate for sheriff.

It seemed that Mr. Goodbread had purchased a negro
from Mr. George, giving in payment a certificate calling for forty-six thousand acres of land. The transac-
tion had occurred some time before with both parties
apparently aware that the certificate was an out-and-
out fraud—but now the Texas Congress had instituted
a republic-wide investigation to sift good paper from
the bad, and this particular certificate had been placed
on the latter list.

Naturally, Mr. George fretted. He wanted back his
negro, and when Goodbread refused to make delivery
the previous master persuaded the slave to run away
and hide in the woods, where he carried him food and
supplies. Now it was Mr. Goodbread's turn to raise
the welkin, which he proceeded to do by broadcasting
through the country the facts about the deal, hoping
that in this way he might hamper Mr. George's chances
for sheriff.

The ensuing scandal held the interest of the entire
settlement; and Captain Jackson, being something of
an outspoken man, took it upon himself to send to
other towns certain letters exposing what he termed
a disgraceful situation of fraud and deceit.

Hence it is not surprising that before long the captain received a warning—in the form of a bullet fired
from ambush as he rode home from Shelbyville. The
slug merely grazed his hand, but it gave Jackson
something to think about. And then he received from
Goodbread a letter making it plain that people who
place a value on their lives should not meddle in the
affairs of others. Jackson frowned for awhile over the

communication, and then called in Eph M. Daggett for a conference.

This young Mr. Daggett, who in later years would help lay out the site of Fort Worth and still later have a street and school named for him in that town, was one of the few citizens of Shelbyville whose reputation really counted. Although still a young man he possessed rare qualifications of judgment which caused others to place high value on his opinions. He called on Jackson, who explained the case, read the Goodbread letter, and asked the future "father of Fort Worth" what he would do under similar circumstances.

"It's no business of mine," said Daggett, "but I can tell you this . . . I once had a difficulty with Goodbread, but I slapped him across the cheeks with a knife and scared him into terms. We agreed then to drop our differences, and that was an end of the matter."

"Well, when I see him I may scare him, too," promised Jackson, "but it will be a damned quick scare. He shan't live . . . he shan't!"

And Goodbread didn't. That very afternoon Jackson, riding into town with a rifle under his arm, found his enemy sitting with an acquaintance in front of one of the stores. The captain rode up . . . the gun in one hand, the note in the other.

"Goodbread," he said, "here is your letter. Git up! I am going to answer it!"

"But I am unarmed," protested Goodbread.

"So much the better," said the other. "Git up on your feet!"

"Charlie, I was mad when I wrote that letter . . .
I was hasty."

"Stand up!" roared the captain.

Goodbread stood . . . to receive a half-ounce ball
through his body. Within five minutes he was dead.

"And now," shouted Jackson, scarcely before the
smoke had cleared the barrel of his gun, "are any more
of the Goodbread rascals in town? If not, bring on
the sheriff!"

The sheriff came, and the former river captain was
taken away to make his bond—in the sum of two hundred dollars—a rather heavy bail in those days for
an ordinary killing on the street. But was this an ordinary killing? It was not. Charlie Jackson had fired
the shot which was to start the bloody Shelby County
war, though none realized it at the time—unless it was
Eph Daggett, a witness to the tragic scene.

In the days which followed Jackson became alarmed.
The high bail and the preparations for his conviction,
he believed, were being carried a little too far, and so
he applied for a change of venue and succeeded in having the case moved to Panola county. The presiding
judge in that court refused the defendant bail and
ordered him to jail, and he might have gone but for
Mr. George, who had just been elected sheriff.

That good man pleaded that the prison was in a
state of dilapidation and suggested that he be allowed
to keep the captain under guard until the needed repairs
could be made. In this the judge concurred, but he had
no sooner left the bench than Sheriff George released
the prisoner and let him go his way.

The regular session of court in Panola still was several months away and although Captain Jackson felt reasonably certain of a fair deal he also felt that nothing could be lost by making sure. Accordingly, he decided that since an epidemic of cattle stealing had broken out in the county, he might serve his fellow citizens creditably by organizing a company of men to deal out justice to the culprits.

Forthwith, he gathered about him a command of thirty men, ostensibly to catch the cow thieves, but actually to furnish Jackson with suitable backing against the day when he should go to trial.

They turned their attention first to a friend of the lately-lamented Goodbread . . . Squire Humphries, who had been accused of going with a newly arrived Missourian to steal a cavvy of horses from Peter Stockman and Black Matt Hays. They caught Mr. Humphries, stripped off his shirt, tied him lengthwise on a tanning log, and then laid on the persuader. They first cut his back to ribbons with the whip, then turned him over and started on the other side, but after the first few blows the victim concluded that he had had enough.

"Let me up!" yelled the Squire. "I'm guilty and I'll let the whole truth come. I'd rather be hung than whipped to death."

Captain Jackson and his men listened to the story, which implicated others, and then after telling Humphries to get out of the country they went out to do a little more "regulating."

Up in the northern part of Shelby county lived a

little community of families known to have been
friendly to the slain Goodbread, and it was in this
direction that the justice-dealing Regulators now
turned the noses of their horses. Jackson rode beside
his lieutenant, Watt Moorman, a young man lately
come from Mississippi. They discussed the business in
hand—a little matter they wanted to take up with Bill
and Bailey McFadden, a man named Bledsoe, and Jim
Strickland, better known as Tiger Jim because he
always used a picture of that beast as warning sign
before he struck an enemy.

On arrival at the settlement, however, they failed
to find any of the men folk at home, and being somewhat put out by this unexpected disappointment, they
contented themselves merely with ordering the women
from the houses and burning every home and stick of
furniture in the community.

Naturally, Captain Jackson was well pleased with
himself as he led his men back home; and naturally,
when Tiger Jim, Bledsoe and the McFaddens came
home they roared like angry bulls. They gazed on the
dying embers of their domiciles and swore an oath that
Charlie Jackson would pay for this day's work . . . and
with his life.

They called together all their friends, and all those
who had been friends of Joseph Goodbread, and de-
clared that the time was ripe for a little "moderating"
in Shelby county. Thus came into being the faction
known as the Moderators, under command of Edward
Merchant—who had killed a man in Alabama and had
come to Texas rather than face trial. Thus the clans

mustered for the fray, each believing itself the proper arm of law and justice . . . but before the Moderators could take revenge for the lately perpetrated arson the case of the Republic versus Charles Jackson was called for trial in old Pulaski.

Meantime both parties had been recruiting, and on trial day the defendant rode to court with one hundred and fifty armed men at his back. Edward Merchant, not to be outdone, traveled by another road with just as many Moderators.

Judge H—— was on the bench that day, and let us digress here for a moment to insert into the record a brief biographical sketch of his Honor by E. M. Daggett, who attended the session and recorded the events of the day in a manuscript now in possession of a relative, Mary Daggett Lake of Fort Worth:

"Judge H—— was another bird," said Mr. Daggett. "Educated as a doctor, he went as a surgeon on a U. S. man-of-war, did some dirt, got discharged, came to Texas and took up the profession of law. He liked a rascal better than an honest man. He got mixed up with the certificate frauds and moved to Harrison county. He became judge of the district court, got drunk, puked on the docket, and General Rusk had to adjourn court for him."

So much for His Honor, the arbiter of the law in the country along the Sabine.

Jackson brought all his men into the court room; but the Moderators, hearing that the judge intended a postponement, kept clear to wait for possible developments.

But let us dip again into the pages of this ancient manuscript, ask the founder of Fort Worth to act as reporter, and describe in his own language what took place in that hall of justice:

"Jackson came into court armed and Judge H——— fined the sheriff heavily for bringing a prisoner into court armed. Jackson jumped up, threw off his arms, laid them on the judge's bench, took off his coat and also his shoes, then sat right down in front of the judge and demanded trial. After some preliminaries court was adjourned until next day at nine o'clock. The judge went out into the country as there was no tavern or stable in Pulaski. Jackson's friends had their wallets as well as their guns.

"Tiger Jim Strickland was said to have been in the cornfield nearby with a good rifle in order to shoot Jackson. The field was ransacked but no Tiger Jim found. Next morning about ten o'clock there came a man who said that Judge H——— was in Marshall. He had told this man he was not going to try Jackson with a hundred and fifty-man mob all around the courthouse making fun of court proceedings."

The case was over insofar as Panola county was concerned. What, then, did our ambitious hero do next? Ever with an eye to business he called his men around him and addressed them in these words:

"There are eight or ten nigger stealers who live in or near this place. They came in yesterday to take a look at me. Now let us take a look at them and carry them to Natchitoches. There is a $200 reward for each of them."

"Good enough!" answered his men, and within the hour seven white men, including the Harrison county judge, were in custody and on their way to the Louisiana city. That was a money making business. The Regulators collected the rewards and returned to Texas; the prisoners, still including the aforementioned county judge, got seven years at Baton Rouge.

As for Jackson and the charge against him, fate had decreed that he should never enter another court room. Following the good example set by the Regulators, the Moderators had formally organized "to sustain the legal tribunals in all efforts to punish the guilty and maintain order and tranquillity." They were preparing to handle in their own good way the case of the former riverman.

Not long after the amusing proceedings at Pulaski they found their opportunity. They learned through spies that Jackson, in company with an inoffensive Dutch merchant named Lour, had gone to Logansport on the Louisiana side to transact some business, and as the two returned home in the swale of the evening a battery of shotguns roared suddenly from a roadside ambuscade.

Jackson and Lour died instantly, their bodies riddled with buckshot. The slayers were Tiger Jim, the two McFaddens, Bledsoe, the lately whipped Humphries and three companions, one Boatright, Henry Strickland, a brother of Tiger Jim, and a fourteen-year-old brother of the McFaddens.

They congratulated themselves on a good day's work, but when they realized what the death of the neutral

Lour would mean, their premature joy turned to fear.
They had not meant to kill the Dutchman, for he was
highly regarded in the county and had held aloof from
either side. The shotgun brigade would have a hard
time explaining that he had merely been in the line of
fire. They knew that the crime would bring dozens of
recruits to the Regulators. Even Tiger Jim's brother
Henry, whose favorite pastime was Bowie knife duel-
ling in a marked circle, was afraid. The band went to
the chief of the Moderators, asked for an escort out of
the county, and sought safety in the canebrakes along
the Sabine.

The news of the chief's death shocked the Regulators. As soon as they heard of it they met, pledged
themselves to track down the slayers, and then selected
a new commander to succeed Captain Jackson.

They chose Watt Moorman . . . thus opening the
way for an era of bushwhacking unequalled, perhaps,
in all the history of the world.

Colonel Moorman, who had come to Shelbyville as
a store clerk, was an enigma; a colorful and fantastic
figure whose counterpart, either in fact or fiction, is
hard to find in the story of any land—unless, per-
chance, he might be compared in some ways to the man
of Sherwood Forest.

He was not, according to the testimony handed down
by those who knew him, a man to stir romantic fancy
. . . not the sort of man who might be expected to
take the lead in this grim sort of open warfare . . . but
even so the Regulators had chosen well in selecting
him to take the place of Jackson.

According to Eph Daggett: "Watt could shoot straighter than any man I ever saw. He was a good scholar, wrote poetry that was real funny, and he had a comical laugh. He would not work or confine himself to any kind of business, was the ideal of his father and mother, played billiards and ten-pins, bruised fellows' heads with billiard cues, rode his friends' horses, spent their money and wore their clothes."

He was at this time about twenty-nine years of age, black-eyed, muscular, and of medium build. He usually wore a half-military coat, and carried belted about his person a Bowie knife and a brace of single-shot pistols. He was versed in Walter Scott and the clannish traditions of Caledonia; he was courting a sister of Eph Daggett, a girl who carried the name of Jane Porter's heroine in Scottish Chiefs. . . . Helen Mar.

He carried a heavy stick with which to cane his minor enemies and, like Robin Hood himself, he carried a hunting horn upon the cantle of his saddle. . . .

CHAPTER THREE

WATT MOORMAN RIDES THE ROADS

The accidental killing of Lour sent the McFaddens and the Stricklands to the canebrakes; the election of Watt Moorman as chief of the Regulartos kept them there . . . for they guessed, and rightly so, that Watt soon would be riding hot upon their new-made trail.

Behind them they had left turmoil. Incensed by the crime, the people of Shelby county were taking sides, and many citizens not heretofore identified with either faction were enlisting on one side or the other. While both Moderators and Regulators recruited, Colonel Moorman called another council, which accomplished two things—a vote of death for the slayers of Lour and Jackson, and selection of fifteen men to act as a squadron of vengeance. Heavily armed, and with Moorman riding at the head, this party left Shelbyville.

On the Trinity river they caught up with five of the fugitives—Bledsoe, Squire Humphries and the three McFaddens. Bledsoe refused to surrender and got a fatal dose of buckshot in the side. The others, after being assured of a fair trial, came out of the house where they had barricaded, and laid down their arms.

The squadron of death now returned to Shelbyville with their prisoners.

"And now," Watt told them, as the party entered town, "you are going to get one of the best trials any set of men ever had . . . the citizens of Shelbyville will act as jury."

An immediate mass meeting was called, and when about three hundred townspeople had assembled Watt opened "court." He simply stated the issue, life or death for the prisoners, and then asked the pleasure of the populace. On a rising vote death was the winner, and the company repaired at once to a nearby clump of trees to carry out the sentence . . . for there could be no appeal from the grim and terrible court of Shelby.

Bill and Bailey McFadden were the first to go. The mob lifted each onto a horse's back, knotted a rope about his neck and tied the other end to a tree limb, but even while these preparations were being carried out Bill cursed his executioners with every oath he could lay tongue to. He called the Regulators thieves and liars, said they were stealing his life, and that they would one day pay for it by wading through blood themselves.

But Moorman's men merely laughed and whipped up the horses. The brothers McFadden were jerked from the saddles, their necks broken. . . .

Then the Regulators turned their attention to Humphries. The Squire said he supposed he deserved death since he had neglected to leave the county after his whipping, but added that he had been persuaded to stay and help kill Jackson.

"I was after you, too, Watt," he remarked with a gay laugh as he was lifted on the horse for his last ride, "but now, instead of me killing you, you are

going to hang me. Well . . . be at it. Let the thing be
done and over with."

The Regulators accommodated him almost at once;
but when it came time for the execution of the fourteen-year-old McFadden boy the avengers, hard as
they were, could not find it in their hearts to go
through with the matter. They considered for awhile
and finally decided that if the lad would tell all he
knew of the Stricklands he should have a pardon.

The boy didn't know a great deal but Regulator
spies, following up several leads, located Boatright on
a plantation in De Soto parish, Louisiana. Thither went
Moorman and his bodyguard, and finding the fugitive
picking cotton they arrested him in the field and con-
veyed him to the Texas side of the Sabine. It was the
intention of the Regulators to take Boatright back to
Shelbyville for trial, but on the way it occurred to
some of them that this was all a useless waste of time.

So it was arranged that one of the squadron members, a former lawyer, should profess friendship with
Boatright and offer him a chance to escape. Accordingly, this man asked permission of Colonel Moorman
to speak privately with the prisoner, and when the
request was granted the 'attorney' took his 'client' a
short distance into the wood.

"This is your chance," he whispered. "Now run!"

Boatright thanked his supposed friend, wrung his
hand, and started. He received . . . as a farewell gift
. . . a load of twenty buckshot in the back!

Moorman tried for days to track down the Strickland brothers in the canebrakes, and although he once

got near enough to shoot Tiger Jim through the shoulder, the brothers got away. The Regulators were to be cheated of vengeance in these two cases. Tiger Jim later crossed the line to Natchitoches, got into an argument with a Louisianan, and received a pistol ball through the head.

A nondescript citizen who styled himself Colonel Shoemaker knocked out Colonel Henry Strickland's brains in a grocery store where Henry was cowing the proprietor, throwing whiskey all over the place, and raving like a wild animal. Shoemaker entered with a deer rifle on his shoulder and Henry insisted on a fight. Shoemaker said he wasn't in scrapping mood and to prove it grasped his deer killer by the barrel and brought the stock down on Henry's head. The lock of the gun entered the brain pan. . . .

Unsuccessful in his attempt to snare the Stricklands, Moorman returned to Shelbyville, where the situation was becoming more tense with each passing day.

The civil authorities were powerless to cope with the situation. They were but mere figureheads elected by one faction or the other, but it so happened that each side managed to keep a friendly justice of the peace in office. One of these dignitaries was a Moderator, one a Regulator, or at least in sympathy and understanding.

There were many citizens who desired to remain aloof from the controversy, but at this time—the early months of 1842—matters had come to such a crisis that more and more men were being compelled in self-defense to unite with one party or the other. If a man refused to join the Regulators he was termed a Moderator; if he refused to join the Moderators he was classified as a Regulator. It developed simply into a choice between two evils—with both factions shouting the rights of man and each believing itself the real stronghold of law and decency.

Moorman's company for the present was in the ascendancy. The Regulator chieftain, ever growing more confident and ambitious, kept possession of Shelbyville with a picked command of armed men. This group, numbering fifteen, followed him everywhere he went; and the citizenry, knowing that the colonel only had to say the word to bring an army to his side, treated him with marked respect.

Moorman controlled not only public affairs, but the grand jury—for whenever that august body met Watt managed to get enough men on the panel to prevent any indictments against his Regulators. Thus he made life, generally, miserable for the Moderators who, being of the weaker party at the time, remained quiet and bided their time.

In short, the former store clerk had become superior to the law. For instance, when the spring term of district court convened it was expected that the names of those concerned in the McFadden hanging would be presented to the grand jury, but when Judge W. B. Ochiltree took the bench he discovered that Watt objected to having his power questioned.

The Colonel obtained a small piece of artillery, mounted it on cart wheels, and dragged it to a spot near the courthouse. There he and his men rammed powder and scrap iron in its throat, trained its muzzle on the building, and hinted to the judge that it might be best to call off the session. Shelbyville, the cannon seemed to say, could run its own affairs.

Ochiltree, however, was not easily intimidated. He mounted the bench, laid a brace of pistols on the table before him, and calmly ordered the sheriff to remove the cannon and arrest anyone who interfered. Colonel Moorman and his friends had not counted on anything like this, but for a reason which will soon become apparent they allowed the sheriff to have his way.

The grand jury then met and District Attorney Royal T. Wheeler, later a justice of the Texas Supreme Court, presented the names of a dozen or more known to have been involved in the hanging bee, but in the end no true bills were returned. There was a reason . . . more than half the members of the jury had themselves participated in the mob! Moorman smiled to himself and went home.

And now we come to one of the most interesting phases in the career of the Regulator chieftain—his romance with Helen Mar Daggett, the sister of Eph M. Daggett.

This sprightly and handsome young lady was esteemed throughout the community, and for some months Watt had been paying court. The girl's family had sided with the Regulators and it was only natural in that time of general excitement that she should take a deep interest in the tragic and thrilling adventures of the colonel. A girl of strong character but possessed of a romantic disposition, she saw in Moorman a

brave and chivalrous gentleman and it was not long
before admiration developed into love. There were
many in the community who attempted to dissuade her
from keeping company with the young man of her
choice—members of Moderator families who sought
to depict Watt as a lawless and a desperate character—
but to these critics she replied that Watt was as good
as any other citizen in Shelby county. She wanted to
know, in substance, if they knew of any one so free
from blame that they could throw the first Shelby
county stone in those troubled times. And it seemed
that none could answer.

Helen Mar Daggett was not to be turned from her
course and so at length the couple were married, despite
the objections of brother Eph. Moorman congratulated
himself. Was it not fitting that he, the greatest feudsman of them all, should take as wife one as thoroughly
steeped as himself in the lore of Caledonian clans . . .
one named for the heroine of Scottish Chiefs? He
didn't know it yet, of course, but her help was to count
for a great deal more than he imagined . . . for the
evidence of her hand was seen in the plans of more
than one battle that he fought in the months which
followed.

Her kinsmen were on the Regulator side and Helen
Moorman believed her husband in the right. Perhaps
he was; perhaps he wasn't—no man of today, looking
back on the events of that tragic era, can say. Conditions, viewpoints, and men themselves, were so vastly
different that retrospection is apt to bring about misunderstanding of cause and result.

Anyhow, it is certain that Watt Moorman dreamed great dreams and looked forward to the day when he should become the most powerful man in all East Texas . . . yes, perhaps in the Republic itself. He primed his pistols and returned to the wars . . .

It is not possible to record here a detailed account of the numerous violent acts which followed, for that would require volumes, but in the succeeding months no man knew what next might occur to disrupt the peace of Shelby county. Men on both sides were dragged from their homes and whipped on charges of various kinds, others were chased from the county, and the gentle art of waylaying became a general practice. Watt used his walking stick to good advantage, too, in these days, soundly threshing a few of his minor enemies. Because of one of these affairs Watt himself was made target for one of the roadside pot-shooters, but in some miraculous manner he managed to escape the hand-hammered slugs manufactured for his special benefit.

And then occurred a difficulty which again threw the entire county into turmoil. It began with a quarrel between two Regulators, Henry Runnels and Samuel Hall. Runnels accused Hall of stealing his hogs. Hall made warm denials . . . a little too warm . . . and forthwith both men armed themselves to the teeth against the time when they could settle scores. But Runnels had an employe named Stanfield and when this man, visiting in Shelbyville, happened to meet Hall on the street, he drew a pistol and shot him through the head. Then he mounted a horse and streaked for

the Louisiana line, hotly pursued by the sheriff and
a posse.

Stanfield, however, failed to reach safety. He had
scarcely crossed the Sabine before the sheriff's men
caught up, took him in custody and carried him to
Shelbyville jail . . . in which Stanfield languished for a
few days, then escaped, stole a horse and left for parts
unknown. Hall's brothers finally trailed him to Mississippi and then to Arkansas, where they hanged him
to a tree and left his body for the wolves.

But in the meantime the killing had caused other
complications. Henry Runnels, while transporting a
load of cotton to Shreveport, was filled with buckshot
by two gentlemen who wandered casually into his camp
and asked for a drink of water.

Now Runnels had been a good Regulator and Moorman's company, as soon as the crime became known,
swore vengeance. They built a scaffold on courthouse
square and took at oath that it would be left standing
until every man concerned in the murder had been
swung from the crossbar. Through a negro servant
of the deceased the blame was fixed on two new arrivals
from the States—two men who styled themselves Jamison and Wickliffe—and upon receipt of this information Moorman and his fifteen rammed heavier charges
in their guns and took the road.

They trailed the pair across the Louisiana line, beat
out the Grand Cane region, and caught one—Jamison,
whom they carried back to Shelbyville as fast as they
could ride.

Jamison confessed as they led him to the gallows.

He hesitated on the steps, told what he knew of the crime, then singled out the village preacher.

"Parson," he said, "that horse of mine is one of the best in the country. See that I get a decent burial and he's yours."

The good pastor accepted the noble steed, watched the Regulators stretch the prisoner's neck, then claimed the body.

Jamison was buried in a cheap pine box, and in his hanging clothes—that is, except for his boots. These the pastor had removed, to give to the negro who helped him dig the shallow grave.

Jamison's confession, in which he told of being hired to kill Runnels, gave Moorman something to work on. It implicated Joseph Hall, Dr. Todd and John M. Bradley, the latter a Moderator sympathizer who had been an enemy of Runnels; but before the Regulators could go out and attend to these gentlemen they had first a situation of their own to face in town.

The hanging of Jamison, without due process of law and in the shadow of the courthouse, appeared to some of the neutral citizens as an intentional insult to the laws which the Regulators had originally set out to uphold—and as a result many of these bystanders now were joining the latent Moderators, which group needed but a little more strength to challenge Moorman's power.

It was a situation which required careful watching but even while the colonel waited, Bradley struck. Taking advantage of the public sentiment, he swore out writs against Moorman and some of his followers charging them with Jamison's murder.

In order to properly and safely serve these papers, which had been issued by the Moderator justice of the peace, the sheriff, something of a neutral in the conflict, organized a large posse which included quite a number of Moderators. Of course this aroused the ire of the Regulators, but Watt and a few of his men surrendered quietly and demanded immediate hearing —but before the justice of Regulators sympathies. That worthy man made short work of the proceedings. He scanned the documents with a knowing look, pronounced them faulty, then ordered release of Watt and all his fellows.

Then the chief of the Regulators struck back. He, in his turn, got out writs charging Bradley, Hall and Todd as accessories in the murder of Runnels. He sent them to the sheriff with the following letter:

"A. Llewelyn,

You have been so damned energetic in attempting to enforce the laws of this county, I hereby forward you writs against your friends Bradley, Hall and Todd. We will now see if you are as persevering in the discharge of your duties as you have recently been. But we will see that you do your duty. If you do not, by God, I'll make you.

"C. W. Moorman."

Colonel Commandant of the Regulating Company, WATT MOORMAN
was an enigma. Like his wife, he was versed in the clannish traditions
of literature; and, like Robin Hood, he carried a hunting horn on his
saddle when he rode forth to fight the bitter East Texas wars. This
picture, now owned by Mary Daggett Lake of Fort Worth, is the first
published of the noted feud leader.

It was now Bradley's turn to give himself in custody. With his friends he surrendered and also demanded immediate hearing—but, of course, in the court of the Moderator justice. A few witnesses were heard and after a little argument it was decided that the crime was committed in Louisiana and that Texas courts therefore had no jurisdiction. The case was quashed.

In a few days the Regulators got one of the Hall boys, James. They killed him as he plowed in his field, and then the squadron of death rode forth to hunt down Bradley who, playing the role of a wise man, had departed suddenly from the county.

But even while he hunted Bradley bad news came to Moorman. He was informed that after a series of secret meetings the citizens of Shelbyville had organized another faction, with Colonel James F. Cravens as the head. Worse than that, the Moderators were enlisting.

Moorman hurried into town to find Cravens and his "Reformers," as they called themselves, in charge of the place. He considered awhile, then sat down and wrote a peace treaty in which he pledged himself as "colonel commandant of the Regulating Company" to lay aside arms and harm no "good citizens," if the opposition would do the same.

The Reformers agreed, and on an evening in mid-July, 1844, both factions signed—but the Moderator group forgot to ask Moorman what he meant by "good citizens."

The next day or two passed peacefully enough,

although Colonel Moorman still was followed by his bodyguard as he went about the county. The chief began making plans, preparatory to a return to power . . . and then he heard that John M. Bradley had been seen in San Augustine.

He sent a spy to investigate.

CHAPTER FOUR

THE RAVEN TAKES A HAND

Under the usual rules of espionage the good spy does not suddenly approach the enemy and stare him in the face—but although this was exactly what Mr. John Farrar did when Colonel Moorman sent him to San Augustine, he still might be considered one of the best among the Regulator secret service men.

Farrar's instructions had been simple. His job was to locate Bradley, learn something of his movements and then report back to Moorman at his camp outside Shelbyville—that and nothing more.

Imagine, then, Mr. Farrar's utter surprise when, riding down a road near Augustine, he came face to face with his quarry, whom he knew only by sight. Imagine, too, his further embarrassment when Mr. Bradley presented his gun, a long-barreled fowling piece, and put the following query:

"Ain't you John Farrar of Shelbyville?"

The spy, his eyes on the menacing weapon, lied.

"No," he said. "I'm Frank Farrar from Arkansas . . . John's brother. I'm on my way to make him a visit. Know him?"

Bradley, with a doubtful expression on his face, raised the fowling piece until the other man found himself looking down the barrel.

"See anything in there?" he asked, and upon Farrar's

35

answer in the negative, continued: "Well, there are twenty buckshot down there hidden under a wad, and if I ever hear that you have deceived me I'll put them all in your carcass."

So saying he rode on, leaving Farrar so badly frightened that he became lost in the woods and did not reach Moorman's camp, twenty miles away, for twenty-four hours. He told Watt the story, together with information that Bradley was in the habit of attending a protracted meeting then being held in the outskirts of the town.

Moorman received the news with no little joy. Here, at last, was a chance to avenge the death of Henry Runnels, and the following evening he took an unfrequented road to San Augustine trailed by four of his men, all armed with shotguns, pistols and Bowies.

Arriving near the meeting house Watt hid his men in the nearby woods, draped a woman's shawl over his head and shoulders, entered the church and took a seat among the women. He peered about the congregation and in a little while located Bradley, who in turn had spotted Watt.

The services went on and both men remained in their places, but just before the final hymn Bradley left his seat and went outside. Watt waited until the closing prayer and then shuffled out with the crowd—to find Bradley waiting just outside the door, his hat pulled down over his eyes, a long coat draped about him.

The crowd was moving slowly and when Watt got near enough to his enemy he drew one of his pistols, ran his arm around some of the others, and fired. The heavy slug struck Bradley in the stomach, just where Watt had told his men he would aim. Bradley staggered backward and squeezed convulsively on the trigger of a short double-barreled shotgun he was carrying, already cocked, under the folds of his cloak. There was a roar as the charge of buckshot peppered the ground, and then Bradley fell.

Pandemonium reigned. Women and children screamed. Men ran about telling one another that Bradley had been slain, and asking who did it. In answer Moorman threw off his shawl.

"Watt Moorman is the man!" he shouted. "Where's your sheriff? I'm ready to go with him."

A man stepped forward.

"I'm Deputy Patton. You can come with me," he said, and together the two started out across the chuchyard. But they had not gone far—not more than fifty paces—before the officer heard something click in the colonel's pocket. He stopped short.

"Watt, I have not arrested you," he said.

"Then you go right on, Patton," said the prisoner, kindly, "I know you don't belong to Bradley's gang of rogues."

The deputy went . . . and Watt, lifting to his lips the hunting horn he carried under one arm, blew a blast that echoed like a trumpet call through the dark East Texas pines. An answering yell came from the men in the woods whereupon the churchgoers, fearing that the entire Regulator army was about to descend upon them, scattered to their homes like frightened geese.

Then Watt blew another blast—the pibroch of another war.

With the fighting fever still upon him he returned to Shelby with great purposes in mind—including plans for execution of those named as accessories in the killing of Henry Runnels. But first, he told himself, he would whip the county into line and establish himself once more as the undisputed king of the district. The Moderators were mustering, Bradley was dead— the treaty already was little more than a worthless scrap of paper.

In the intimidation project Moorman had immediate and remarkable success. He raised a standing army of one hundred men. He terrorized the opposition. He made his more prominent enemies take to the woods and, as one witness of the day described it, "caused them to curse the day they set foot on Texas soil."

And then, according to the records left by the Moderators, he planned the master stroke of all—an audacious and almost inconceivable program which, if he really was serious about it, had to be carried out while his star remained in the ascendancy.

He planned, according to his enemies, a junta—an armed revolt to overthrow the Republic of Texas, and take for himself the presidency then occupied by General Sam Houston!

Moderator literature still extant makes a great point on this subject, but nowhere in any of the manuscripts left by Regulators can any mention of it be found. There is no doubt that Watt, like Caesar, was ambitious, but no one can say now what was in his mind in those days.

If, however, he did entertain any rebel ideas he counted on three factors—first, his own faithful following; second, neutral citizens who would welcome any change rather than put up with existing conditions; and third, the Regulator forces in nearby counties. Shelby, it may be well to mention, had been the original home of the "regulating" but now the practice had begun to grow in other counties along the line . . . Harrison, Panola, Sabine, Nacogdoches and San Augustine.

There were those who doubted that Watt would attempt to extend his terrorism campaign, but the Regulator chief was determined.

He called a meeting for the night of July 28, 1844, at the home of Matthew Brinson and there he caused to be organized a "provisional committee" for the formation of a new county government, with himself as the commander-in-chief of the armed forces.

With the house guarded by one hundred men, the committee selected officers, and then inquired as to the next business to come before the house. Watt didn't hesitate; he stepped in and handed to the "new government" a list of twenty-five names.

"The men listed here," he explained, "are disturbers of the peace, and there can be nothing but war as long as they remain in Shelby county. I want them proscribed, with orders to leave within fifteen days!"

At this drastic move a murmur of protest went up from some quarters. Eph Daggett, the future "father of Fort Worth," was strong in his argument against it. He said that he knew the county was in a state of turmoil, and that he believed the Regulators were doing much more in the interest of law and justice than the Moderators, but at the same time he believed this measure a bit too strong.

Colonel M. T. Johnson, who later was to found Johnson's Station, another Tarrant county town, also took the floor in opposition.

"Many of you," he said, "believe you can resolve and notify these men to leave by resolutions and hostile demonstrations . . . but you will have them to fight. So lick your flints, keep your powder dry, and don't deceive yourselves. I fear the consequences; it is a bad move."

There were many like Daggett and Johnson, mature and level-headed men who saw the folly of Watt's more high-handed plans, but they were in the minority. The younger men voted them down and drafted a decree containing the names of the twenty-five—including Sheriff A. Llewelyn and Colonel James F. Cravens, leader of the Moderators. It warned the proscribed men to get out of the county in the specified time "or be considered outlaws."

Then Colonel Moorman called on his bodyguard and ordered the members to deliver the notices personally to each of the twenty-five on the list. Now this was touchy business, considering the time and place, and the squadron moved with the utmost caution as it approached the first home, that of Thomas Haley.

This Haley was a very careful man and when he

happened to glance from his windows and see strange
men stealthily approaching his domicile in the darkness, he got down the long rifle, loaded it with two
slugs, and went to the stable to barricade himself.
He didn't know what it was all about but he was
taking no chances, and as the nocturnal visitors drew
near Haley rested the rifle over one of the stalls and
cut down at one of the moving figures. Of the two
slugs in the rifle, one ball drilled through the skull of a
horse while the other broke the arm of a Regulator.
And, as Mr. Daggett says in his memoirs—"some leaving took place followed by a cussing match."

Thus discouraged the Regulators went back and told
Moorman the story of their adventure. He decided
then on another plan. The list would be made into a
handbill to be posted on the door of the county courthouse, an idea that was carried out next morning.

But if the Regulators expected the sheriff and Jim
Cravens to accede without a struggle they were sadly
mistaken. Those two gentlemen boiled with righteous
rage when they saw their names among those posted.
They sounded a call to arms, and the Moderators and
the Reformers began to rally in the town.

News of this reaching Moorman's ears, he prepared
for battle. He sent a detachment in all haste to build a
fort on Buena Vista road about three miles west of
Shelbyville on the Beauchamp farm, and then he dispatched a courier to Harrison county's Regulators
asking them to come over and join in the festivities.

As a site for the fortification the Regulators selected
a log house to which a large amount of lumber recently

had been hauled in preparation for new buildings which were about to be started. These boards they stacked about the house and fence in such a way that an adequate defense against buckshot was provided, and then the Regulators began rallying to the rendezvous.

Meanwhile, in Shelbyville, Colonel Cravens had received information on the movements of the enemy and he sent a company of fifteen men to reconnoitre, ordering them to shoot without warning any member of the proscribing committee they might chance to meet. On the scout they met one, shot him from his horse and continued on their way. They rode to within two hundred yards of the Regulator fort, exchanged a few shots, and then returned to report the situation to Cravens.

The Moderators started laying in supplies and ammunition and two days later, on the fourth of August, they marched against the enemy.

Colonel Cravens decided to attack from two angles. He sent half his men to storm the fort from the rear, while he advanced with the remaining half and opened a brisk fire from the front. The Regulators, however, made a warm return and Cravens retreated, praying for a piece of artillery, even if only a small cannon. He settled his Moderators in the tall timber and for several hours each side sniped at the other but did no serious harm.

In numbers the odds were slightly in favor of the Moderators—who had two hundred and twenty-five men against the sixty-five Regulators holding the log house—but the latter force had the better position. But let Mr. Daggett describe conditions in the fort.

"We had a house, a good yard fence and a lot of flooring plank, all of which made breastworks. We hung up sacks and blankets in some dogwood trees and these drew their fire over our heads. The Regulators, being surrounded, found that the Moderators had sent word to Shelbyville that we were being killed in heaps and that they thought this would be the last battle of the war. Forty-four women who had sons, husbands, brothers and sweethearts among the reported dead came at a gallop to hear the last dying words of their loved ones. They looked wild. They passed the enemy camp and came on to ours. How their countenances changed when they saw only a few wounded and all the others in good spirits!

"After the women rode back the Regulators tried to draw a charge. One of the men climbed up on the fence, clapped his arms like wings, and crowed like a rooster. He kept this up for some time and then a bullet clipped off part of his scalp and knocked him into the enclosure.

"We could not see the enemy," continued Mr. Daggett, "but we could hear them calling their men in line for a charge. One of our good sharpshooters killed a man at two hundred and eighty paces. The Moderator had been shooting nearly all day at the little four-foot split boards our man was using for a breastwork. A dozen balls had entered the boards, but when they went through one they flattened out a little and by the time they went through another they were too flat to enter the next . . . so this man had quite a pocketful of slugs. He finally got his man when the latter exposed part of his body while loading. He fell from a forked oak.

"They (the Moderators) tried three times to make the charge, but the men were too prudent. Had they made it we would have cleaned them up. Our men lay flat on the ground with double-barrel guns, rifles and pistols, and had rail fence cracks to shoot through, crib logs to shoot over. We reserved most of our fire for close work."

Quite a neighborly little row, that fight at Beauchamp farm. Watt himself wasn't in the fort at the time; he had gone to muster new recruits, and to meet a hundred men coming from Harrison county.

Night drew on and the men on both sides suffered from thirst, but the only spring in the vicinity was between the two forces and in range of both parties. Consequently, under cover of darkness Cravens fell back to a creek two miles away, and while he was gone the Regulators abandoned the fort and headed for Hilliard's Spring, about fifteen miles in the other direction. There they met the hundred men from Harrison county and thirty more that Watt had managed to muster. The Regulators felled trees about the spring and waited for a new attack. Morning brought none— but it did bring two hundred more recruits from Harrison.

Colonel Cravens laid low for a few days awaiting reinforcements. He received fifty from San Augustine and a few from Louisiana, and then he sent out a spy company to locate the enemy. These riders at length returned and Cravens, after hearing their reports, marched his men toward Moorman's camp but stopped at an old log meeting house two miles from Hilliard's Spring. Sentries were posted and a meal was started . . . and then a strange thing occurred.

A woman on horseback was seen approaching. She rode like the wind, spurred through the sentry-line, and inquired for Colonel Cravens.

"Why, that's Watt Moorman's wife!" someone shouted, and men came running from all points in the camp to learn what her business might be. Eagerly they crowded around as she explained.

"Colonel Cravens," she said, "I have a complaint to make against some of your men. A short distance from this camp I was fired on, and narrowly escaped with my life. I believe you to be an honorable gentleman . . . one who would not allow an unoffending woman to be put in peril because she is connected with your enemies, and I hope that for the honor of Texas these men may receive punishment which will prevent a similar occurrence in the future."

"I am deeply mortified, madame," apologized Cravens, "if any of my men have forgotten themselves to that extent. I'll do what I can about the matter."

Cravens and Helen Moorman had by this time become the center of an interested crowd. Even the attention of some of the sentries was attracted. She said she knew the colonel would see the thing clearly, and then she thanked him and rode away.

She had scarcely passed the last sentry post, however, before the Regulators opened fire! Almost too late Cravens saw the intended trap . . . saw how the clever and daring Helen Mar Moorman had wilfully distracted his men while her husband's army crept up for the attack! She had led the charge in the greatest battle of the feud!

The Moderators managed to save themselves, and for that reason the spot where the incident occurred is known to this day as Helen's Defeat. The Moderators scattered, some taking refuge in the meeting house, some in the canebrakes along the creek, and just in time.

Watt Moorman, raising his hunting horn, sounded the signal for another charge.

An afternoon of sniping followed. Splinters flew from the sides of the old log church as the home-made slugs struck home; lead swished through the tops of the tall cane.

It was a confused scene and more than once both Moderators and Regulators, having no distinguishing marks, opened fire on detachments of their own men. A dozen men fell in that fight at the meeting house, and many more might have died had not Moorman sounded the retreat when he did. He blew one blast on the horn and the Regulators began falling back to Hilliard's Spring.

Watt had just received alarming news—that General Sam Houston was about to take a hand in the battle. The Raven, visiting at the time in San Augustine, had heard of the conflict and had ordered several militia companies from nearby counties to enter Shelby and stop the disturbance.

"We will have to disband for awhile," Watt told his force. "Each man take the open course and take care of himself."

The company scattered. Watt himself hurried north to hide—and rode squarely into one group of militia-men, whom he had approached in the belief that they were Harrison County Regulators.

The Raven himself, from his headquarters in San Augustine, directed troop operations and within a few weeks many other leaders from both factions were arrested and required to make peace bonds in Shelby-ville. There came, too, this proclamation from San Augustine:

"It having been represented to me that there exists in the county of Shelby a state of anarchy and misrule—that parties are arrayed against each other in hostile attitude contrary to law and order —now, therefore, be it known, that I, Sam Hous-ton, President of the Republic of Texas, to the end that hostilities may cease and good order prevail, command all citizens engaged therein to lay down their arms, and retire to their respective homes. Given under my hand and seal.

SAM HOUSTON."

The general kept troops in the town for several months, and thus one of the bloodiest wars in Texas history drew to a close. After the departure of the militia old animosities sometimes flamed anew, but only in a modified form. The War with Mexico really wiped out the last vestige of emnity between the feudists, in the opinion of Mary Daggett Lake, great-niece of Colonel Moorman's wife.

"In 1846," she points out, "Colonel M. T. Johnson raised a company from the former Regulators, and Major Alfred Truitt one from the Moderators, and they fought side by side in the Mexican war as units in Colonel Wood's regiment of Texas Volunteers. They distinguished themselves at Monterrey and in other battles and it is probable that they satisfied their blood lust in the fighting, because peace reigned after they returned to Shelby county."

As for Watt Moorman—he went to live at the old home of his parents near Joaquin. His whole world, it seemed, had fallen down about him. Gone were his dreams of revolution; gone, too, were his friends— even his wife. But that had been his fault . . . he had deserted her in the days of brooding after the defeat.

He went no more the road to Shelbyville, but he did make freqeunt trips across the Louisiana line to Logansport. On one of these journeys he quarreled with a Dr. Burns and after an exchange of threats they met at a landing on the Sabine. The doctor, who was carrying a double-barreled shotgun, saw Watt first. . . .

The coat the Regulator chieftain was wearing that day is now in the possession of Mrs. Lake, but it is hardly a coat that any man would care to wear . . . its back being too well-filled with buckshot holes. She has,

HELEN MAR MOORMAN, named for the heroine of Jane Porter's Scottish Chiefs, was versed in the traditions of the Caledonian clans. Otherwise, she might not have led the *Regulator* charge at Beauchamp farm. This photo was taken in Fort Worth during her later years.

too, one of the pistols found beneath his body when they turned him over on the Sabine wharf.

* * *

One thing more—out in Mt. Olivet cemetery in the northern section of Fort Worth there is a headstone which bears the name of McKee, and the casual stroller in that haven of the dead is like to pass it by without a second glance . . . little suspecting that underneath the mound of earth it marks rests one who helped to make a thrilling page in Texas history.

Fort Worth knew her as Mrs. William McKee. She was Helen Mar Moorman when she led the Regulator charge at Beauchamp farm. . . .

CHAPTER FIVE

HELL ROARIN' ROSE

Captain William Pinkney Rose was a fighting man. Even the most bitter among his enemies were willing to concede that point, and that's why they called him what they did—Hell Roarin' Rose.

Lean, six-feet-two in height, with the eye of a hawk and the muscles of a panther, he was an amiable sort of individual in the milder moments of his life, but on the other hand decidedly was a man to avoid when anger chanced to stir his soul.

Like Captain Charlie Jackson, our hero in a previous chapter, the title which he bore was valid. A native North Carolinian, he had established something of a military record before bringing his wagon train across the Sabine to take up residence in the Republic of Texas during the winter of 1839.

He had commanded a company of United States troops in the War of 1812 and he had learned his more important lessons under the able tutelage of General Andrew Jackson and Captain Jean La Fitte of Barataria, boldest of the South Coast buccaneers—for Captain Rose had been behind the cotton bales when those two hearties whipped the British in the Battle of New Orleans.

But even if he had won his spurs in the military field, it was not until he had been elected commandant of the

Harrison county Regulators that the former Carolinian earned the more vivid and distinctive title of Hell-Roarin' Rose.

At this point it must be borne in mind that the period whereof we speak was contemporary with that which marked the beginning of Watt Moorman's rise to fame and glory in the adjoining county of Shelby—the early days of 1842.

As previously pointed out, Shelby had been the original home of "regulating" and, no doubt, it was Watt's signal success in the shotgun handler's lively trade which tempted the civil government students of neighboring districts to duplicate the system.

Consequently, it wasn't long before other counties—like Harrison, for instance—soon found themselves possessed of opposing factions who called their organizations Regulators and Moderators. Watt merely set the style for that section of the country, commonly caught in the grip of universal chaos and lawlessness.

Harrison county, to explain the situation briefly, simply became a sideshow for the main event—one single offshoot of the great feud which raged a few miles to the south—and since conditions were so similar in every corner of that blood-soaked land this addenda to the narrative will concern itself principally with that grim incident which brought about the death of the Republic's first Secretary of Navy, Robert Potter.

But first—a bit of background:—

When it was decided by the good people of Harrison county that the time was ripe for a Regulating company of its own, what better man could be found to head the

organization than Captain William Rose? He was
elected at the company's first meeting, held in Marshall,
and it wasn't long before the fireworks started.

The captain, never one to let much grass grow under
his feet, set out at once on the trail of a band of Negro
stealers. He caught them on the Trinity, laid on the
hickory limb an ample number of counts, and then
galloped home to seek out other evil-doers. In this he
found little difficulty. Back after back felt the searing
cut of the swishing rod, man after man was ordered to
gather up his personal belongings and make an exit from
the community . . . and before the passing of many
months the captain had earned full right to his title of
Hell-Roarin' Rose.

He had in his company many of the leading citizens
of Marshall—men like Isaac Hughes and George W.
Rembert, prominent planters, and the Reverend James
Gill, the Methodist parson of the town—and though
animosities had flared from the very start, it was the
slaying of two of these favorite lieutenants that heaped
new fuel on the fire.

Two men arrested by the company as thieves lured
Rembert to his death. Gaining the planter's confidence
they hinted that they could lead him to a hangout of
cattle stealers, and when Captain Rose sent Rembert
and two others to make the arrests Rembert was fatally
wounded as he walked into a farmhouse trap carefully
planned by the two informers.

Hughes was working in his field when an opposition
party approached and ordered him to surrender. Being

near-sighted, he merely laughed and attempted a joke with the Moderator leader.

"How many men in your party?" he asked.

"About thirty," came the reply.

"I can whip that many alone," said Hughes, with a laugh.

He never laughed again . . . for the charge of buckshot he received in his chest killed him instantly.

Reece Hughes, his brother, evened scores, however, a few days later. He learned the name of the Moderator leader, sought him out in Port Caddo, and shot him down on sight.

Thus one incident led to another in the district until Harrison county bid fair to make itself a second Shelby. To record all the deeds of violence which tended to disrupt the peace in and about the city of Marshall during those days would fill a sizeable "saga of the shotgun", but even though the war never did assume the proportions of that carried on by Colonel Moorman, one episode does stand out in bold relief—the shooting of Colonel Potter.

Bob Potter, as he was familiarly called in the country about Caddo Lake, where he made his home, was one of the signers of the Texas Declaration of Independence.

He had come to Texas in 1835 from North Carolina, where he had served in the legislature. He settled at Nacogdoches and had been in the country but a short time when elected delegate to the convention which framed the Declaration at Washington-on-the Brazos. In the *ad interim* government he was elected secretary of the navy, and after San Jacinto he served in the cabinet of the Republic until after the inauguration of President Sam Houston. Then he resigned, went back to East Texas, and settled on a headright grant of 4,605 acres on the banks of Caddo Lake.

But Mr. Potter hadn't been on his new estate long before he became involved in the controversy between the Regulators and the Moderators, choosing the latter side because he happened to be at outs with his neighbor, Hell-Roarin' Rose.

At first Potter and Rose had been more or less friendly, but when the former secretary of the navy sought the hand of one of the Rose girls in marriage the captain let him know at once that he did not look upon him favorably as a suitor. Captain Rose said that he had received unpleasant reports regarding certain phases of Potter's life in Carolina—and then he intensified the feeling of emnity by supporting the candidacy of John B. Denton, who was running for Congress in opposition to Potter.

But as things turned out Denton—who later had a North Texas county named in his honor—was killed by Indians, and Potter went to the Texas Congress. There he started a bitter campaign against Captain Rose in connection with the latter's leadership of the Regulators. He denounced Rose as an outlaw, and at length succeeded in securing a requisition for the arrest of the captain—dead or alive.

Then, with Congress in adjournment, Colonel Potter came home to see what he could do about putting the requisition into effect. He gathered about him a company of twenty men and in the dawn of a July morning in 1842 started for the captain's house. Just before sunrise he put a cordon of men around the place, then went to the door and demanded the surrender of Rose.

The captain, however, was an early riser, and he already had gone into the timber to instruct a gang of negroes in a clearing project he had started. Mrs. Rose answered the door in response to Potter's call.

"The captain isn't here," she said.

"And you couldn't get him if he was," put in Preston Rose, a son.

"We'll search the house, anyway," said Colonel Potter and he pushed past Mrs. Rose and entered, his men following.

The group went through every room and then, not finding any clue to the captain's whereabouts, Potter went outside and fired a volley of shots into the air, hoping that the sound might bring Rose to the scene in the belief that his family was being massacred.

But the shots only served to warn the captain of his danger. He looked toward the house, saw the party of armed men and suspected their purpose. Therefore, he threw himself on the ground and ordered one of his negro servants to pile brush wood over him. The negro, old Uncle Jerry, fell to with a right good will, and by the time the Potter party had mounted horses to start in their direction Captain Rose was completely concealed under the brush.

Potter, at the head of his twenty, rode up and asked the negro if he had seen Rose.

"No, suh," said Uncle Jerry. "Master done gone som'mers."

Potter looked at him closely, and just at that moment an old rooster, which had wandered into the woods, caught a glimpse of the captain under the brush pile. The bird started an immediate crowing and scratching, as though trying to inform the entire world that the heap of brush held a secret known only to himself.

Potter eyed the fowl suspiciously. Rose scarcely dared breathe, and he was more than mildly relieved when Uncle Jerry nonchalantly stooped, picked up a clod, and hurled it at the offending bird. Potter tarried for a moment and then reluctantly rode away.

Now the first act of Captain Rose, as he crawled sweating from the brush pile, was to take up a club and run down the rooster. The bird properly dispatched, he set off for town, swore out a complaint against Potter, and secured a writ for his arrest on a charge of trespass. Then he passed certain information to members of the Regulating company and went home to bed.

Captain Rose was up and about long before daybreak the following morning, and when he left his house he found a sizeable party waiting for him in the clearing outside. With this group, nine in number, he took the road for Potter's place and upon arrival stationed his men in convenient spots about the house.

At daybreak one of Potter's men, Hezekiah George, came out to reconnoitre and ran squarely into Captain Rose, who was loitering near the corn crib. George turned and ran, but Rose raised his shotgun and fired. George received the contents of both barrels in the seat of his trousers, but he survived the wound—to be known thereafter as "Old man Rose's lead mine."

Inside the house Potter heard the firing and jumped from his bed. He didn't need be told what it meant, and without waiting to dress, he dashed from the house and ran for Caddo Lake, one hundred yards away.

Hotly pursued by the Rose party, the colonel made a running dive into the water, hoping, perhaps, that he could swim beneath the surface long enough to make his escape—but Rose and his men knew that they had him.

They cocked back the hammers of their guns and waited at the water's edge.

Finally, Potter could stand the strain no longer. He simply had to have one little gulp of air. He allowed himself to rise to the surface for a second, but that second was all that the Rose men needed—and there was a deafening roar as Potter sank again.

A few days later an old man sat lazing in his boat, wondering why the fish refused to bite. Suddenly something popped up to the surface beside his scow . . . something gruesome, terrible. The panic-stricken old man dived overboard, splashed ashore, and scrambled up the bank. Then he ran from the scene as fast as his trembling legs could carry him, and shouting at the top of his voice.

"The devil has riz! The devil has riz!"

But he hadn't . . . it was only the body of Robert Potter, late Secretary of the Texas Navy.

Captain Rose and his son-in-law, John W. Scott, together with the other members of the party were put under arrest, but after a hearing in Nacogdoches were released when the prosecution admitted lack of sufficient evidence.

Nothing more came of the affair, though it seemed that common gossip of the time credited Scott with firing the fatal shot. The practice of bushwhacking warfare continued in Harrison, but never did it reach the heights attained in Shelby. You have learned, in the preceding chapter, how it all came to an end—with General Houston's militia breaking the feud after the battle of Beauchamp farm, an affair which, as you may remember, was helped along by many of the Harrison Regulators. The death of Robert Potter, however, attracted more outside attention than any other incident in all the East Texas controversy. Even Charles Dickens, visiting in the United States at the time, read about the case in the newspapers and he mentioned it in his volume of American notes.

Hell-Roarin' Rose survived the bitter conflict. Several years later he died a natural death and was buried at Scottville.

The name of the Secretary of Navy later was perpetuated by the state of Texas. When, in 1876, a new county was created out of Bexar, it was seen fit to call it Potter—"in honor," so said the papers memorializing the event, "of a distinguished citizen of the Republic of Texas, and a signer of the Declaration of Independence."

THE TAYLOR-SUTTON FEUD

CHAPTER SIX

INTRODUCING MR. WINCHESTER

A smile of deep satisfaction spread itself over the face of Mr. Nelson King as he rapped discreetly on the door which led to the offices of his boss.

In all the city—in all the state of Connecticut, perhaps—could be found no happier man than Mr. King, for as superintendent of the New Haven Arms Company he was experiencing the realization of a dream. After months of toil he had reached his day of triumph, and even now he held that triumph in his arms, a long object of blue metal and brown wood which could be identified at once for what it was—a rifle.

But what a rifle! It was something entirely new, something which touched upon perfection in the gunsmith's trade, a creation so ultra-modern both in design and theory that it upset in every detail the popular conception of that weapon. Was it any wonder then that Superintendent King was pleased as he opened the door marked private and entered to lay before his chief this superlative product of his skill?

Nelson King had succeeded where others had failed. He even had outdone the master of them all, the far-famed Tyler Henry, whose perfection of the old Volcanic had brought about the gun which bore his name —a weapon already popular on the buffalo runs of the West, an arm with which two regiments of skirmishers were equipped as they had marched with Sherman to the sea.

But the Henry rifle hadn't been enough; and the light of a great pride was in the superintendent's eyes as he put his creation down before the boss. This, his manner seemed to say, was indeed the masterpiece.

"There you are, Mr. Winchester," said King, "the fastest shooting, hardest driving rifle in the trade . . . tested, proven, and ready for the market. "

The man behind the desk eyed the weapon critically, took it in his hands, tried the mechanism, examined the polish of the wooden stock—and then he, too, smiled in satisfaction.

"King," he said, "this rifle may revolutionize the industry. Mark my word, this is the gun they've been waiting for in the southwest, in such states as . . . well, say Texas, for example."

But how much brighter might have been that smile if the firm's president could have peered for a moment into the future. The name of Oliver F. Winchester was about to become famous, about to become a by-word over half the North American continent, and still later over the world itself. That morning in the New Haven Arms factory he had made himself sponsor for a brand new implement of social service . . . an implement of retribution, death and vengeance which for a time would rule the West and then in the end help put it on the way to civilization, and keep it there.

The creation on his desk really was the thing for which the great Southwest, and Texas, had been waiting . . . the Winchester rifle, Model of 1866.

In the eyes of many this little incident may lack proper significance. It may be regarded merely as a sign of natural progress in the art and science of invention, an event as matter of course as the development of the steamship and the locomotive—one of those experimental accidents which keep the world forever on the move—but whatever may be said on that score, one fact remains . . . the innovation helped to change in no small part the customs of a country.

Now you may wonder what all this has to do with the story of Texas feuds. Well, there is such a thing as coincidence. It really couldn't have been anything else, but it so happened that the first successful repeating rifle made its appearance at a propitious time, at a season when the western world was on the doorstep of what might be termed the "Bloody Decade," a period through the 1870's when murder, riot, and sudden death made up the rule rather than the exception; and in this strife the State of Texas held the center of the stage.

And so this tale can not properly take its course without some gesture of tribute and appreciation to those inventive geniuses whose efforts aided in no small way to add some modicum of color to its chapters. Without Nelson King and Oliver Winchester some of the more startling episodes, some of the more red-tinged portions of the story, might have been lost forever . . . for theirs were the hands which helped to launch a brawling time of tumult on the way.

The Southwest, and Texas particularly, did need rifles. Death itself could not have provided a setting more favorable to the business of the armament makers.

The Comanches and the Apaches were raiding in the West, swooping down on the scattered settlements to leave behind a trail of blood and fire and death.

Armies of Mexican cattle thieves, under command of General Juan Cortina, were raiding on the Rio Grande, slipping across the line to take entire herds and then fight their way home again under the guns of small but daring bands of Texas Rangers.

The country was overrun with thugs and bandits, discharged Confederate and Union soldiers striving to make an honest living—through horse stealing and cattle theft. The cattlemen, attempting to reassemble wild herds neglected during the Civil War, were hiring gunmen to protect the leavings of their fortunes.

The State of Texas itself, experiencing the trials of reconstruction, was for a time in the hands of a carpet-bagger governor, E. J. Davis. Discontent held the land in its grip, politically, socially and economically.

John Wesley Hardin was leading roving outlaws through the South, emptying jails and terrorizing citizens; Sam Bass was in his hey-dey in the North, killing men and robbing trains; everything, everywhere, had gone wrong. A letter which a district judge in a remote section of Texas sent to the Adjutant General emphasizes the condition:

"I am well satisfied," he said, in part, "that if the Legislature does not provide some material aid to civil authorities in the crime-stricken districts of the frontier, that the courts will be closed, that civil law will be suspended, that anarchy and lawlessness will ensue, and that there will be a receding frontier whose boundary line will be marked by the sword, the pistol, the shotgun and the rifle."

Another thing—the vital and important question of free range. It did seem as though the gods or dissension had excluded nothing from the scheme. Blame coincidence, if you will, but already families were quarreling among themselves over rights of pasturage, calling one another cattle thieves and worse . . . everything, in fact, within the profane range of the accomplished frontiersman.

Thus it was that the beginning of the "Bloody Decade" found the stage set for a repetition of events such as those which occurred when the Regulators and the Moderators fought it out in the early 40's. The question of free range and cattle thievery—justified or not—furnished the excuses and the background in most cases. Of more significance is the fact that the temperament of the people was right.

It was for that reason, perhaps, that the Taylor-Sutton controversy, one of the most outstanding of all Texas feuds, involved—like the Shelby County War —not only immediate families but hundreds of others before it reached its dramatic climax. All the greater Texas feuds were like that . . . not so much family affairs, but community "enterprises."

So it was in the Mason County War, and in the Horrel-Higgins affair—both launched on charges and counter charges involving cattle.

So it was in the San Elizario salt troubles, that brawling, seething episode of hate and murder which ended with a firing squad down on the Rio Grande. . . .

And so it was in the state's one great political feud, which began with ballots and ended with Winchester bullets on the ground outside the Fort Bend courthouse down at Richmond.

These feuds, however, did not make the "Bloody Decade"; rather they were contributing factors, events which furnished the major highlights of the era. As previously pointed out, it was a day when property had no sacred value, when human life was cheap. The temperament of the people had reached the breaking point, and the time was ripe for settlement of gathering scores . . . for rifles in the dusk.

And Oliver Winchester's Model 1866 had been perfected just in time. . . .

CHAPTER SEVEN

THE GUNS OF VENGEANCE

On a fine evening in the spring of 1869 a social entertainment was scheduled for the town of Clinton, at that time the governmental seat of DeWitt County.

It was to be a gala affair, with all the belles and beaux of the community in attendance, and even before sunset the hitching rail in front of the courthouse presented a scene of happy confusion . . . for through the courtesy of Judge Henry Clay Pleasants the entertainment was to be held in the district courtroom.

Ranchmen and farmers from the outlands tied their teams to the hitching rack while wives unloaded cakes and pies and chickens from the hacks and surries. Children, caught by the spirit of holiday, romped and played on the square, and spurs jangled in the dust as the inevitable cowboy swung from the saddle to drop his reins and join the happy throng.

And then in the midst of all this gaiety, Buck Taylor and Richard Chisholm came to town . . . to play the principal roles in an event not contemplated by the program.

Buck Taylor was a member of one of the most prominent ranching families in the county; Dick Chisholm was his cousin; and like others among the young bloods of the district they wanted to have a part in the festivities at the courthouse.

But even as they dismounted before the building
two shots rang out, two figures fled in the failing light,
and before the crowd had time to realize what had
occurred Buck Taylor and his cousin Dick lay dead in
the street, each drilled through with a pistol bullet.

Of course, the usual period of excitement followed,
but the good people of DeWitt County were not the
sort to let a thing like gun play disrupt the evening's
program. The bodies were taken away and the entertainment proceeded as scheduled, the attendance
materially increased by the number attracted by the
tragedy.

But, quite naturally, all conversation centered upon
the affair, especially since rumors were heard about the
courthouse that Bill Sutton and Doc White might be
involved.

If that were so, some of the older men ventured to
predict, more trouble might be reasonably expected,
for it was common knowledge in the counties of De-
Witt and Gonzales that the Suttons and the Taylors
were at outs, and there were worried frowns upon the
faces of those who knew the inside story of the trouble.
All too well they recognized a situation filled with
powder—and with the fuse already burning short.

The Taylors and the Suttons at that time were, without doubt, the largest cattle families in that section,
and both had stock upon the free and open range. In
that lay the root of the entire difficulty. When members
of the respective families came home from the Civil
War they found, as other returning Texas cattlemen
had found, a country filled with wild, unbranded stock,

great "maverick" herds to which their own neglected cattle had contributed. And so, as a matter of course, maverick branding became the fashion on the ranges.

Now the Taylors and the Suttons had not been home long before they fell into disagreement over cattle on certain portions of the range. It was, at first, just a quiet sort of little quarrel such as any two families might engage in, but as time went on something occurred to heap fire upon the smouldering coals and bring about a bitterness which only blood could satisfy.

Jack Helms had been appointed United States marshal in that district of Texas and he took office with a determination to put a sudden and effective end to branding evils and range quarrels. As his chief deputy he chose one Joe Tumlinson, himself a cattleman, and incidentally a friend of the Suttons. Joe was ambitious. He thought he could solve the problem easily, and it wasn't long until there appeared in DeWitt County a band of men who called themselves Tumlinson's Regulators, an idea taken perhaps from the style set by Watt Moorman in the '40s.

But the Regulators got away to a bad start by killing a cattleman who happened to be among the bosom friends of the Taylors. Then, in a street quarrel, Helms stopped a .45 slug fired by another friend of the Taylors—none other than young John Wesley Harden, who already had more than thirty killings on his list. In this way the dispute between the two families began to involve others. Jim, Buck, and Billy Taylor began receiving callers, sympathetic friends from all parts of the country who pledged their full aid in case the Tay-

lors ever needed it. Men called, too, at the homes of
James and William Sutton, where similar pledges were
made.

The famous Taylor-Sutton feud was on, though
few people seemed to realize it, or worry about what it
would mean—unless it was the stern-visaged, outspoken jurist who held the bench of the district court
—Judge H. Clay Pleasants.

The judge, who with his wife and nine-year-old son
Robert attended the entertainment in the courthouse,
was plainly perturbed. He feared that the evening's
shooting scrape might start the guns of vengeance roaring. He hadn't long to wait . . . the victim being a rider
for the Sutton outfit.

And then came an event which transformed the
county into an armed camp. The opposition faction,
as a beginning, caused the arrest of Coots Tuggle,
Mason Arnold and one of the Taylors, Scrap by name,
on a charge of cattle theft. The sheriff, W. J. Weissegar, was a careful and a cautious man and upon arrival
in Clinton and upon hearing that a mob was forming
to take his prisoners, he hastily organized a protec-
tionary posse large enough—or so he thought—to
guard the men from violence.

But the sheriff soon discovered he had miscalcu-
lated, and before dawn the lifeless bodies of Scrap
Taylor, Tuggle and Arnold were swinging from the
limb of a tree in the little cemetery above the town.

Clinton, of course, turned out to view the triple
horror, and among the spectators was a lad on his
way to school.

"It was a scene I never have been able to forget, those bodies swinging in the wind," says that boy—today Judge R. A. Pleasants of Houston, chief justice of the first district Court of Civil Appeals. "And I shall never forget how my father, the district judge, worried over the affair."

The district judge had plenty of cause for worry. No man could say that the Sutton faction had any part in the affair, no man could say that they had so much as encouraged the mob in the grim task it had performed—but the fact remained that both the Taylors and the Suttons were mustering to full strength, with each side gaining new recruits from among their friends.

Scores, even hundreds took sides according to their inclinations, and men went about heavily armed, ready to shoot at the drop of a hat. With each passing hour the situation grew more tense and Judge Pleasants, ever a bulwark on the side of law and order, realized that some decisive action must be taken at once if the community was to be saved from a reign of terror and blood unequalled since the Shelby County War.

For a moment he considered calling upon the governor and the adjutant general for assistance, but even while he pondered there came a crisis which, owing to its nature, could not wait upon arrival of state troops or Texas Rangers.

Judge Pleasants was informed that the Suttons, rallying with their friends at a point south of Clinton, were riding toward the town with the intention—now that they held the advantage, or believed they did—of preferring cattle thieving charges against certain members of the Taylor aggregation.

The Taylors, however, were not people to let a challenge go unheeded, and simultaneously with the first report the judge received another—to the effect that the Taylors were on the move, that even then they were on their way to Clinton with a party equally as strong to see that the Suttons did not carry out their purpose.

The judge, of course, knew that this wouldn't do at all. Why, if the two parties met in Clinton a single word, if uttered only in jest, might bring a battle in the streets. So Pleasants, dropping for the moment his attitude of meditation, went forth to meet the trouble on the half-way ground—but first taking the precaution to arm himself with a double-barreled shotgun. DeWitt county was going to remain on the side of law and order, at least while H. Clay Pleasants sat upon the district bench!

The Suttons already had reached the courthouse when the judge, coming from his home, arrived on the scene. The Taylors, all with blood in their eyes, were just fording the river that skirted the town.

Sullen and silent, they rode in while the Suttons, nervously fingering the trigger-guards of their Winchesters, watched from the shadow of the courthouse. Citizens of the town, their nerves already ragged from the strain of recent days, scattered for cover—but not so His Honor the district judge!

That grand old man of the bench, whose hair already was graying about the temples, was by far the coolest man in all the town of Clinton. He cocked back both hammers of his shotgun and stepped out into the open ground between the two contending factions!

"Gentlemen," he said, "we have had enough of this futile business. We are not barbarians, and while I am judge in this district I intend to see that peace prevails in DeWitt county."

Cooly and deliberately, he shifted the shotgun in his hands.

"It is my suggestion," he added, "that all parties concerned leave town immediately . . . we'll have no trouble here."

It was the sheer audacity of the act, perhaps, which turned the trick, for the leaders of both factions seemed to realize that here was a man who meant business. They agreed, more by sign than by word, to let matters rest for the present and take separate roads out of town. The courage of a single man, in the face of stupendous odds, had turned impending tragedy from its course.

The jurist watched the parties leave and then, with a tired sigh of relief, went home to rest—but not for long. He was dealing, and no man realized it more fully than he, with a passion which already had passed beyond control. The judge was soon to take the field again, his shotgun on his arm. For the opposing factions had scarcely crossed the river before they broke the truce, each side firing a few random shots as they took their separate roads—which, strange to relate, both led to the city of Cuero.

Now this was something that Clay Pleasants had not bargained for, no stipulations as to route having been made, but even so he was not in the least surprised when late that night he was awakened from his sleep to be told that both groups had reached Cuero at approximately the same time, and that the prospects appeared bright in that city for the battle which the town of Clinton had missed.

He didn't say much. He merely dressed, went to the barn, saddled his horse, and asked his son to bring his shotgun. Then he set out for Cuero with Sheriff Weissegar and a hastily organized posse.

The situation there was none too cheerful. The city had taken on the appearance of a rallying point for the clans. At least a thousand heavily-armed men, from all over DeWitt and Gonzales counties, had gathered, each ready and willing to side with the friends of his choice.

Bill Sutton himself was on hand. He had taken up headquarters in the local hotel and from there he was watching the various moves of the Taylors, who had established themselves in the town's one and only lumberyard. Both sides were taking advantage of the situation to muster all additional recruits possible.

Only an hour before the arrival of the Clinton posse Bill Sutton, dropping in at a Cuero grocery store, had found Gabriel Slaughter sitting on the counter.

"If you're my friend and want to help me, Gabe," he said, "now's the time for you to do it."

"You know me, Bill," replied Slaughter, who was a nephew of the judge, and from that moment on his fate was cast with the Suttons in an alliance which, in the end, was to bring him to his death. In this manner the new recruits took their places in what was to prove an open season for bushwhacking.

When Judge Pleasants and Sheriff Weissegar arrived with the posse both sides had settled down to watchful waiting, each loath to attack, each hoping that the other would be first to take up the reins of battle. Sizing up the situation, Judge Pleasants, wise beyond his day in the science of pyschology, knew that now was the time to strike.

"There are many good men in Cuero who are neutral," he told the sheriff, "and so let us deputize a hundred or so and arrest every man identified with either faction. It's the only way to break the trouble, for if a fight really starts there'll be no stopping it."

But the sheriff shook his head in doubt.

"I'm afraid to try it, judge," he said. "It's a good plan, but if we try to arrest every armed man on the streets we'll only be forcing trouble, and a lot of good men will be killed. It's not worth it, Pleasants, it's not worth it."

The judge argued, but his pleadings fell on deaf ears. The sheriff believed it best to let matters take their course, and then meet the situation when it came.

"Then I'll wash my hands of the whole affair," said Pleasants, at last, "I'm going home." And he mounted his horse, set his shotgun before him across the saddle and jogged off toward Clinton, leaving the sheriff to handle the difficulty in his own way.

The predicted fight didn't come off at all, though the two factions remained in their positions for two days.

The grand finale was, in fact, more humorous than
tragic.

Bill Sutton, field marshal for his group, had received
word at the hotel that he could expect at any time a
reinforcing party of nineteen or twenty men, and that
when they arrived they would hoist a white flag on a
hill outside the town to inform him of the fact. On the
morning of the third day Sutton saw the flag and decid-
ing on strategy, ordered forty or fifty of his most active
warriors to mount and follow him on a pretended flight
from the city.

The effect on the Taylors was exactly what Sutton
had hoped for. Sensing victory, half a hundred men in
the lumberyard scrambled for their horses and set out
in pursuit of the Suttons, who kicked in their spurs and
made the retreat appear as realistic as possible.

The Taylors had not seen the white flag and almost
too late they discovered their mistake . . . for the
Suttons, immediately after contacting their reinforcements, turned and became the pursuers instead of the
pursued. Without a shot being fired by either side the
Taylors reached the slaughter pens on the prairie half a
mile outside the town. There they hurriedly dismounted,
turned loose their horses, and entrenched with their
Winchesters ready for action.

It was a tense moment, and one random shot might
have set the fireworks going, but the Suttons, riding
buckety-buckety behind their opponents, likewise were
cautious. They pulled up as the Taylors reached the
stock pens and, just out of rifle range, they settled

down to fight a battle which was waged with words instead of bullets.

All afternoon a shouted argument went on across the patch between the forces, and after threshing out first one question and then another, the leaders finally agreed that for the sake of themselves and the country at large it would be best to call the whole bitter business ended.

Thus the "battle of Cuero" came to a close with both factions going home to lay aside their arms; but, as later events were to prove, the principals couldn't so easily put aside their thoughts. Something still rankled.

Even through the peaceful months which followed Bill Sutton and his brother James felt this; and they decided that since trouble was certain to arise again . . . trouble probably suicidal for all concerned . . . they had best sell out everything they owned and depart from the country, never to return.

James was the first to dispose of his property, and after the last acre of land had been sold and after the last cow had been converted into cash, he loaded his family into wagons and departed for West Texas, DeWitt county saw him no more.

Bill found his close-out transactions a little more involved and it was not until the early part of 1874 that he was ready to make his exit from the troubled land. Then, with Mrs. Sutton, he went to Indianola to board a boat . . . his old friend of the Cuero controversy, Gabe Slaughter, traveling with him.

They arrived by carriage at the coast town on the afternoon of March 11, and they went at once to the

wharf where the Steamer Clinton was preparing for
departure. Slaughter and Sutton walked up the gangplank, with Mrs. Sutton walking between them holding
to her husband's arm, but as they proceeded down the
deck toward their cabins some instinctive sense of impending danger caused Gabe to glance backward over
his shoulder. He stopped short and shouted a cry of
warning.

"Look out, Bill!"

Sutton whirled. There on the deck, not twenty feet
behind him, stood Jim and Billy Taylor, their revolvers
already drawn!

Sutton and Slaughter reached for their own guns,
but the Taylors were a shade too fast.

"Here's something for you!" cried Jim Taylor, level-
ing down with a pistol in either hand. He squeezed the
triggers, and Bill Sutton dropped dead on the deck, one
bullet through the head and one through the body.

A split second later Gabe Slaughter lay beside him, a
half-cocked Colt within ten inches of his hand . . . his
face smashed by an echoing shot from the revolver of
Billy Taylor.

Mrs. Sutton screamed, and swooned. . . .

Jim Taylor picked up Sutton's gun, a white-handled
Smith and Wesson, and then hurried with his brother
down the gangplank to mount their waiting horses, a
brown and a sorrel, and ride away.

The guns of vengeance had scored a double marker
—one for Buck Taylor, another for Scrap.

The officers of the law at Indianola went after the
two slayers but they only got Billy, who was fortunate

enough to win his freedom a short time later when the great hurricane of that year blew down the Indianola jail. He was arrested later by Marshal Russel Brown in Cuero and at that time a white-handled Smith and Wesson pistol was found in his possession. Billy said that the weapon had once belonged to his deceased Uncle Buck, but when Taylor went on trial in Calhoun county the prosecution showed that Uncle Buck passed violently away prior to the patent on the revolver, and offered to the jury the theory that Billy must have received the weapon from Brother James, who at that time was frequenting parts known only to himself.

The jury gave Bill ten years, but the sentence later was reversed by the Court of Criminal Appeals on the contention that Taylor had killed Slaughter by mistake while trying to wing Sutton.

In the case of James Taylor fate had arranged something more exciting than the monotony of a court trial. . .

CHAPTER EIGHT

MURDER AT MIDNIGHT

When news of the shooting on the coast reached
DeWitt county the friends of the Suttons, quite naturally, began to sweat under the collar. They fairly itched
to get after the Taylors again, but since Jim Taylor was
so conspicuously absent they had to wait in patience
for the settlement of scores. The opportunity came
during the Christmas holidays.

Jim and two of his followers, Winchester Smith
and a man named Hendricks, chose that festive season
to make a call on friends at a farm near Clinton. Now
Jim had to be very, very careful as he went about the
country but through some channel known only to themselves the Sutton faction—now kept alive by friends of
the original family—learned of the Yuletide party and
planned to add certain surprise elements to the occasion.

And so it came to pass that Taylor and his two
friends suddenly found their haven surrounded by enemies. They tried to make a run for it; tried to escape
by making a wild dash through the fields—but the Winchesters of the Suttons shot straight. The three died in
the cotton rows.

But even before the fatal affair had reached its climax
District Judge Pleasants was on his way to the farm.
Tipped by some one who had seen the Sutton party
approaching the trap, he left his office hurriedly in the

hope that he might possibly arrived on the scene in time to prevent bloodshed, but he didn't. Let the present Judge Pleasants describe the events which followed.

"Just before the killing," says the Houston man, "I heard that trouble was coming and, knowing my father's attitude in the matter, I went at once to look for him. Not finding him in his office I hurried on toward the reported scene of the impending conflict, but before I could reach the farm I heard the volley which killed Taylor, Winchester Smith and Hendricks. Some of the bullets, in fact, whistled through the trees over my head.

"By the time I arrived at the cotton field quite a crowd of townspeople already had collected. They were standing at the fence, afraid to go farther. I began looking for my father, and not seeing him, became alarmed. Over across the field I could see the members of the Sutton faction still lingering at the spot where their three victims had fallen . . . and then I spotted my father. He was striding across the field two rows at a time straight toward the Suttons, who had him covered with their rifles.

"But despite this threat he didn't pause. He walked directly up to the group and in a voice that could be heard even by those peering through the fence, delivered one of the most scathing and bitter rebukes of its kind I have ever heard. And then, still ignoring the rifles, he passed around the killers, turned his back on them, and walked over to view the remains of Taylor, Smith and Hendricks. The Sutton party left, and then my father returned to the fence and asked some of the bystanders to help him move the bodies. One negro volunteered,

but not a single white man . . . for the fear of the feudists was strong upon the public in that day and time."

It was that same sense of fear which kept the scales
of justice empty. In all the country, perhaps, there was
but one man who went his way unafraid, and that man
was H. Clay Pleasants—but standing as he did, alone,
what could the tall district judge hope to accomplish?

The very thing which he had sought to prevent had
become reality. The two factions, though without an
actual Sutton or an actual Taylor in the respective leads,
had developed into grim "lodges" with a large section
of the county's citizenry divided into warring camps.
The two groups had retained, merely for convenience,
the names of the two families whose differences had
started the trouble.

Other killings, directly or indirectly traceable to the
feud, followed—and then something occurred which
marked the beginning of the end for the dark and
bloody business.

A company of men, allegedly members of the old
Sutton party, killed an outsider—the community physician, a man who stood, as doctors should, on neutral
ground.

And more than that they took him from his deathbed, at a time when they knew he had, at the most, but
a few more hours to live.

But retribution rode behind the deed.

*   *   *

Dr. Philip Brazell lay dying, and he knew it. He had
been physician to the people of Dewitt county too long

not to know a fatal disease when he encountered it, and already he had broken the news to his wife and four children, who remained almost constantly at his bedside.

Outside the farm home the leaves were beginning to fall from the trees, for it was late September of 1876, and as the doctor watched the sunset from his window he knew that before the last brown patch had floated down upon the wind, he too would be gone. Tonight he felt weaker. The strength slowly was ebbing from his body, and he was glad that he had sent one of the boys into Clinton that afternoon to ask County Assessor William Grafton if he would come out on the morrow to draft a will.

Night came on, and with the chores done and the supper finished, the family retired . . . for rural folk in that part of the country went early to their beds. Theodore and Sylvanus, two of the sons, slept on the gallery; Mrs. Brazell, a daughter and one son, George, in the house with the doctor.

It was some time after ten o'clock when the Brazell hounds began to bay in the yard, and as the younger brothers on the gallery rubbed the sleep from their eyes they heard some one out in the darkness shout "Hello!" Theodore and Sylvanus got up, pulled on their pants, and asked who called, and what was wanted.

"The sheriff," said a voice from the yard, and then a group of men advanced to the porch and ordered the boys to come along with them. The two young men, confronted in the middle of the night by a band of masked men, were of course startled, especially so when one of the leaders said that they had come to search for a man they believed to be hiding on the premises. They asked who was in the house, and Theodore answered that it was occupied only by members of the family.

In the meantime the entire family had awakened and Mrs. Brazell, at the request of her husband, had lighted two lamps—but let us go to the records of the court for her story. According to volume eight of the Court of Criminal Appeals reports, she later testified that:

". . . . . Some one on the outside said: "Surround the house, boys." One man, whom the others called Mr. Sheriff, came into the house. At first Mrs. Brazell thought he was Mr. Calloway, a deputy who lived nearby, but found afterwards that he was not. The men outside said: "Mr. Sheriff, search the house," and, speaking to the inmates, said: "Don't be alarmed; we are after someone, but we have no idea he is here; we won't hurt a hair on your head." Some one of them shouted: "All of you come out here, you women folks; put on your clothes and come out of that house"; and kept shouting: "Old man, get up and come out of there; come out, old man." Dr. Brazell got up and went out, and George went out without his hat, shoes, or coat, and the man called "Mr. Sheriff" searched the house; and then George and his two younger brothers were allowed to come in the house and put on their clothes. . . . . ."

But to brief the lengthy verbage of the appeals opinion:

The doctor and his three sons were ordered from the house and Mrs. Brazell, standing by the door, watched the party, numbering seven or eight besides the members of her own family, disappear in the darkness. Within ten minutes she heard a series of shots and she went into the yard and hallooed to the party not to do any more shooting. Answered by silence, she returned to the house . . . to wait. The shooting had occurred after eleven o'clock but it was near one when she opened the door to hear from two neighbors that both her husband and George had been killed.

She then went to the scene of the shooting, several hundred yards away, and viewed the body of the doctor. The body of the son was found about thirty-five yards from that of her husband. Both had been shot.

It was not until later in the morning that Theodore and Sylvanus came home. They had witnessed the slaughter of their father and brother, and the tale they told was rather incoherent. After being led away from the house, they said, George had told their captors: "If you are going to kill one of us, kill us all." Then the firing started and the younger brothers took to their heels. Theodore made his getaway under a barrage of pistol shots; Sylvanus ran, climbed a tree, and hid himself in the leaves.

Both the boys testified that seven men participated in the killing. More than that they named them—and those names tallied with names which Mrs. Brazell said that George had whispered in her ear before being led away to his death.

The Brazells hurried to Clinton to tell the tragic story and to make accusations. The mother and the children gave a detailed account to the authorities and the blame was fixed—on a certain element surviving from the old

Sutton faction; but in the light of events which followed this point has remained unsettled.

News of the double killing aroused the community, for none of the citizens of Clinton who knew the physician could advance a motive for the affair . . . and even to this day the real reason behind the deed remains a dark and puzzling secret.

There appeared to be nothing in the doctor's life which might merit such action—unless he possessed some secret that these men feared. Were they afraid that the man of medicine, since he was on his deathbed, might reveal that thing—whatever it might be? The citizens of Clinton could only guess, and one guess was as good as another.

Even in later years, when the Court of Criminal Appeals had occasion to review the case, that high tribunal could only hazard a guess as to motive. It did, however, bring out this plausible theory—that Dr. Brazell and his son were killed by mistake, the opinion pointing out that one of the men indicted was a deputy sheriff who "had in his hands for execution a writ for the arrest of Theodore Brazell and William Humphries" issued upon the instance of a man named Hardin who claimed that the two had threatened his life. The supposition of the court, then, was that the party had formed as an official posse to make the arrests and that the killing occurred through some unexplainable misunderstanding.

But to return to the day following the killing—September 20, 1876. Clinton was aroused, but no citizen more thoroughly than H. Clay Pleasants. The district judge paced the floor in silence as he listened to the story of the children, and then he sent a cryptic and pointed message to the governor at Austin.

The communication brought results within a week—in the form of a heavily-armed party which rode into Dewitt county and pitched camp on a hill overlooking Clinton. The group was made up of twenty-seven men, and they were a hard-bitten cold-eyed lot—young men, booted and spurred, each carrying a brace of six-shooters at the waist and a Winchester rifle in the saddle scabbard.

On the morning of their arrival one young man of Clinton—one whose name, so it happened, was on the Brazell death list—approached the judge on the street.

"Listen here, judge," he said, in an angry, surly voice. "I want to know what these Texas Rangers are doing in town."

"I can tell you that, suh," replied Pleasants, looking his questioner squarely in the eyes. "They are here at my special request. Dewitt county is about to experience a cleanup, and Lieutenant Hall and his men are here to do the job."

A sudden calm seemed to fall over Clinton, for Lieutenant Lee Hall's fame had spread before him. He and his men had just come from the Mexican border where, under command of that brave blade, Captain Leander H. McNeilly, they had established a singular and sanguine record in their dealings with Mexican cattle thieves. Clinton waited, and wondered.

Judge Pleasants lost no time. He immediately called the grand jury and the evidence in the Brazell murder case was presented. And the grand jury, in turn, wasted

no time. It returned fourteen indictments, two each for
the following men—William D. Meador, Jake Ryan,
James Hester, Dave Augustine, Charles H. Heissig,
Joe Sitterlie and William Cox.

The warrants for arrest were placed in the hands of
Lieutenant Hall and his Rangers.

Now it so happened that the legal event coincided
with a social affair involving one of the men named
in the indictments. Joe Sitterlie was taking a bride—
the daughter of a farmer who lived a few miles west of
Cuero—and that night the happy union was to be cele-
brated with a dance and supper at the farmhouse.

Lieutenant Hall, though not invited, was aware of
this, and hoping to snare all his birds with one cast of
the net, he made plans to attend the gay party.

Mustering his men in the dusk, he slipped quietly out
of Clinton and took the road for Cuero.

CHAPTER NINE

JUSTICE TAKES THE BENCH

When the Rangers arrived at the farmhouse the wedding party already was in full swing. The bride and groom already had said the traditional "I dos" and out through the doors and windows of the house floated the lively music of a fiddle band.

The dance was on, and the resulting noise and confusion, tending to put the participants off their guard, suited Hall's purpose admirably. He deployed his twenty-six men around the house, at points of vantage deep enough in the shadows to escape detection—and then he advanced alone toward the doorway. One man, Bill Meador, was standing on the gallery and with a start he recognized the uninvited guest.

"What do you want here, Hall?" he demanded.

"I want you, Meador," replied the lieutenant, who knew the man. "I want you and six others. Will you hand over your gun, or must I take it?"

"We'll have to see about that," answered the other. He stepped into the room with the officer following at his heels. "Boys," announced Meador, in a voice loud enough to be heard above the din of the music, "we've got visitors . . . Hall and the Rangers!"

The dancing stopped and a hush fell over the dancers.

"Yes," said the lieutenant, "we've come to take the following men. . ." He read the names from the warrants, and then waited for some reaction from the crowd.

"How many men you got?" came a voice from the dance floor.

"Twenty-six," said Hall, "and they have the house surrounded."

"Well, we got more'n fifty," said the voice. "I guess we'll have to fight it out."

The lieutenant smiled.

"That'll be fine boys. That's a part of our business, you know, and we'll be more than glad to indulge. Get your women and children out of the way," he advised, "and we'll get started. I know my men'll be pleased."

He stepped to the door and shouted to his Rangers:

"They're getting the women and children out of the way, and so when I give the signal start raking the gallery and windows with your rifles. You fellows with shotguns move in closer."

At this juncture a tall man in a long-tailed black coat sprinted through the door and scurried away in the darkness.

"Let him go," Hall shouted to the guard-line. "It's only the preacher, and the knot's already tied."

This, needless to say, was sweet music to the ears of the Reverend J. T. Gillette. The Methodist parson, since the marriage rites already had been read, saw no reason why he should linger longer in that house. At first he had counted on staying for supper but now, strangely enough, he had lost his appetite.

This diversion, however, served a purpose. It gave the wedding guests time to think things over; it gave them opportunity to size up the lieutenant and realize he meant business.

Meador was the first to capitulate. He took his revolver from its holster and placed it on a table; and then, one by one, the remainder of the wedding guests stepped up and followed suit. This business out of the way, the bride herself came forward with a request. After all, she said, a girl's marriage did count for something . . . and wouldn't the lieutenant be kind enough to let the party run its course?

Lee Hall laughed and gave his sanction. The band struck up and the dance went on—as merrily as though nothing had occurred. Even the Rangers participated in the wedding supper, coming in by pairs to the feast, then returning to the guard line outside the house.

Then the cold December dawn—and it was a weary company of men that the Rangers led away to Clinton after Hall had warned the stay-behinds that he would meet any attempt to rescue by "killing first the prisoners and then the attackers." No attempt was made and the party reached Clinton without incident.

Instead of taking his captives to the jail, Lieutenant Hall marched them directly to the courthouse, where Judge Pleasants already was waiting to receive them. The proceedings were brief.

"Your Honor," said Hall, "I have arrested forty-two men. I am not acquainted with them all, but I presume the court will know the ones wanted under indictment."

"Yes," said the judge, "I know them all."

He remanded to jail those under charges, then set

the others free. The hearing was over . . . but not for long.

While the prisoners were being kept under guard their friends hired some of the best-known attorneys in that section of the state—E. R. Lane, Sam C. Lackey, John Stayton and others. Habeas corpus proceedings were started at once.

The judge took his own time about the cases, but he heard them one by one until the last was reached, and then came the day when he would render his decision on the granting of bail. It was a tense moment for the town of Clinton, and citizens from all over Dewitt county, sensing that one of the most famous court battles in local history was about to occur, jostled and pushed their way into the courtroom . . . and nearly all with shooting irons, for no man could predict just what might happen before sunset. Even the judge's sixteen-year-old son Robert, the present appeals court justice, sat in the room with a six-shooter on his hip. And, of course, all the former members of the two old factions were present.

The tenseness of the situation was somewhat augmented by reports that Judge Pleasants had received threats—and he had. Only that morning he had found one on his desk, a note warning him that unless the accused men were granted freedom on bail he would be shot from the bench.

A detachment of Hall's Rangers shouldered through the jam and stationed themselves in the front of the courtroom as His Honor took his place. A low buzz of comment ran through the room, and the bailiff rapped for order.

The judge, after seating himself, reached for his pen and began scribbling on a sheet of paper—the decision which would decide the course of law in DeWitt county. And in all that throng of spectators there was not a man who doubted, as he watched the firm set of the judge's mouth and the steady movement of his hand, what that verdict would be.

At last the judge was through with his writing. He laid the pen aside and rose to his feet, and as he did so six Texas Rangers advanced to the platform and stationed themselves at the bench, three to a side. Then they faced the crowd, each officer pumping a cartridge into the barrel of his Winchester. The judge cleared his throat.

"The business of this court is concluded," he said, "but before adjournment I have a few remarks to make, especially to these prisoners and their friends.

"DeWitt county has become a disgrace to the state of Texas, and there are men within sound of my voice who have helped make it that . . . murderers, bushwhackers and assassins. It is not necessary for me to review the history of the strife responsible for this condition . . . all that is too well known . . . but I do want to say that in Clinton and DeWitt county the reign of lawlessness is over.

"However, before I render my decision in this case, one thing more—the foreman of this grand jury has received letters threatening him with death, threatening him with violence for bringing Rangers here. I have this to say . . . the responsibility for bringing the Rangers to Clinton is mine, and mine alone. I asked that they be sent here when all other means of enforcing civil authority had failed."

He reached for the paper on his desk. A deadly silence fell over the courtroom. The Rangers, with their Winchesters, waited.

"The substance of this paper," said the judge, "is that these defendants shall remain in custody. Bail will be denied."

A ripple of suppressed excitement swept over the room, but the bailiff again rapped for order.

"The jail in Clinton is none too secure," added Mr. Pleasants. "The prisoners will be taken to Austin for safe keeping."

And then he adjourned court.

Finis had been written to one of the greatest feuds in Texas history, and principally through the efforts of a single man—H. Clay Pleasants, who had made the law once more a real and living thing.

The crowd filed slowly from the courtroom and in the crush at the door Lieutenant Hall and young Robert Pleasants, who were walking together, overheard a remark from one of the spectators:

"It's hard to find a more determined and hard-headed man than Judge Pleasants . . . when he thinks he's right."

The lieutenant turned about and faced the man.

"You're correct about that," said the Ranger, "and the funny part about it is . . . he's always right."

But what of the prisoners? Lieutenant Hall's men

took them to the blacksmith shop, had them ironed, then escorted them to Austin in pursuance of the court's orders.

At the December 1877 term of the district court of DeWitt county, a severance having been granted, defendants Dave Augustine and James Hester came to trial for the murder of George Brazell and were acquitted. The prosecution in the same case was dismissed as to Charles H. Heissig. On the same day Judge Pleasants, on his own motion, changed the venue as to the other defendants to the county of Bexar. The opening paragraph of that document, entered December 29, 1877, had this to say:

"In this cause, the State of Texas v. William D. Meador, Jake Ryan, Joe Sitterlie and William Cox, charged with the murder of George Brazell, upon motion of the judge presiding, H. Clay Pleasants, and for the reason that the judge is satisfied that there exists in this county influences resulting from the terrorism prevailing among the good people of the county which will prevent a trial alike fair and impartial to the accused and the State, it is ordered that the venue in this cause be changed from DeWitt county to the county of Bexar, in the Twenty-Second Judicial District of this State."

Cox, Ryan and Sitterlie, after having severed from their co-defendant Meador, went on trial in San Antonio the following April before Judge G. H. Noonan. Convicted of murder in the first degree, an appeal was taken on the grounds that the indictments had been faulty because they read "against the peace and dignity of the statute" instead of "against the peace and dignity of the state."

The opinion of the high court said: "For the reason that illegal and inadmissible evidence was allowed to go to the jury, over objections of the defendants, and because the indictment is fatally defective, the judgment of the court below is reversed and the case remanded."

The defendants made bond and the case never came to trial again. Meador died before they got around to him.

As for Judge H. Clay Pleasants, he became in later years chief justice of the First District Court of Civil Appeals, over which he presided until his death in 1899. Today, in the judicial chamber of the court at Galveston, his picture looks down from the wall upon the desk of his successor—his own son, Robert, who watched his father break the bloody feud.

MRS. BILL SUTTON, seated, was holding her husband's arm when he was shot down on the Steamer Clinton at Indianola by James Taylor. The girl in the picture is a daughter, born two weeks after the tragedy. This old photograph comes from the album of Mrs. Sutton's cousin, Mrs. Floy Scovill, of Fort Worth.

CHAPTER TEN

THE SWEEPINGS OF A FEUD

Deep in the Warloupe Mountains of New Mexico, in a remote hill crevice which went by the name of Dark Canyon, a young Texan lay on a blanket and labored over the composition of a letter.

It was important, this communication, for it was going to his sweetheart—the girl he had left behind him when he set out from the Pecos country to seek his fortune in the West. He wanted to tell her not to worry; that he, like so many other young Texans, was finding a bonanza in the lawless atmosphere created by the bloody Lincoln County War; that he was, in fact, doing quite well.

Laboriously and stiff-fingered he scribbled on, paying little attention to the side remarks which came from some of the ten men lying with him in the rendezvous; and a few weeks later a girl over in West Texas received the following *billet doux*:

"Dear——: I will write you again. I am now about five hundred miles from where I written you last. This is headquarters for my gang. I have got ten men with me, the best-armed and best-mounted outfit you ever saw. There are war going on here between two strong factions, and we have got an independent scout of our own. We just got in off a raid and made it pay us big. Darling, I am making money fast, but I see a hard

97

time ahead and am troubled to death about you. If I had you here I would be the happiest man on earth. We are 100 miles from the nearest postoffice.

"Darling, on the 20th day of August Gross and McGuire got into a fight, and McGuire shot him just below the heart, and I shot and killed McGuire. He never spoke after I shot him. We buried him as nice as we could, and sent Gross into the settlements where he is being well treated. I think he will recover. Bob is still with me and is the same old Bob. Darling, I want you to write to me when you get this. Let me know all the news and how you are getting along, and let me know whether you will come or not.

"Darling, you can come to me and I can't come to you. I never can be contented without you. I am satisfied you would like this country, that is, about Fort Stanton. That is where I expect to live if you come, and if you won't come I don't care where I live. If you can come let me know so I can fix for you, darling. All I am working for is yours, if you will come. You know you are the joy of my life. Darling, if you need any money let me know and I will send it to you. Let me know when you can come and I will meet you at Trinidad, at the end of the railroad, and bring you down to Fort Stanton.

"Darling, I have got two of the finest mares in the territory. We have got a big lot of cattle and horses on hand now that we are going to start to sell in a few days. Oh, how I wish you were here. You would look like a child in six months. This is the finest watered country on earth, and the best climate, cool nights all summer. Darling, I have got a Navaho blanket for you that is worth $75, the prettiest thing you ever saw. Baby take care of yourself and be sure and write.

"From your loving one,

"S. Z._____."

That letter, still preserved in the files of the adjutant general's office at Austin, shows how more than one Texan learned his lesson during the Bloody Decade; how they went to a school of outlawry in another state and then came home to start a "university" in the higher and more vicious curriculum of crime.

The territory of New Mexico in the '70s was indeed a fertile field for training. It had become at that time a great cattle country, almost rivaling Texas, and quite naturally it had drawn to it many stockmen from the Lone Star state . . . and where stockmen went thieves were sure to follow. And the thieves followed thither principally because New Mexico had no Rangers —because the law was held, as a usual rule, in the hollow of each man's hand.

Thus it had become something of a happy hunting ground for those young Texans with get-rich-quick ideas . . . although in the end the migration from the West of Texas resulted in more corpses than millionaires. But while they lasted they did their part in making a success of the Lincoln County cattle feud, which brought into prominence such fast-triggered gents as Mr. William Bonney.

This Billy the Kid was a bold buckaroo. His blazing revolver, employed to such terrible advantage in the controversies between the cattle kings and outlaws of

the area, already had blasted out the lives of more than
a dozen men. His story—too often told for repetition
here—already was known in every corner of the wide
frontier.

More than once he had crossed the Texas border
with stolen horses, to sell at Tascosa and other cowboy
capitals where men weren't so particular about a bill
of sale so long as the horse itself was good. And the
Kid, meeting many men and having become something
of a popular hero, tempted others to follow in his foot-
steps on the road to fame and fortune.

With the Kid at the top of the deck there wasn't
room, of course, for many other aces in the game,
but the hero-worshipping attitude did explain many of
the "independent scouts" such as that referred to in
Mr. S. Z.'s letter to his girl in Texas. This young
man appeared, however, a bit more fortunate than
many of his fellows, for it is to be noted that he mentioned having on hand "a big lot of cattle and horses
that we are going to start to sell in a few days." Where
did this consignment of livestock go? Well, Texas is as
good a guess as any.

Some of these immigrants into New Mexico made
good, but more of them did not, and it wasn't long
before the Prodigal Sons, finding no pot of gold at
the rainbow's end, began drifting back to hunt the
fatted calf in Texas . . . some from economic neces-
sity, some barely two leaps and a jump ahead of a
sheriff's posse or an opposition gunman. Thus Texas
got back not only its own, but a varied assortment
of freebooters from other climes . . . as though the

state wasn't having enough trouble with the home talent.

This element . . . the sweepings of a feud . . . caused immediate trouble, the seriousness of which was pointed out in a letter written by Allen Blacker, judge of a West Texas district, to Adjutant General Steele.

"There can be but one road leading through the settled portion of this district," he wrote, "and that can justly be termed a highway of criminals and tramps seeking new fields of crime, or fleeing fugitives escaping from punishment or pursuit from crimes already committed in other states, ready and willing to take other chances in the lottery of felony and outlawry and add another page of infamy to the annals of crime in Texas."

He reviewed in brief the reign of outlawry in New Mexico and cited instances of criminal forays across the Texas line into his district:

"They have depredated on the people of this district and have found a convenient asylum in that country (New Mexico), where the courts are closed by mandate and the execution of civil law suspended. Threats were made to shoot the judge on the bench, and attorneys, officers, jurors and witnesses likewise threatened. Men have been called to their doors and shot down, shot in the houses and through the windows, shot in the back, wherever they might be, for expressing an opinion in behalf of law and order. This killing continued until no man felt safe anywhere and was compelled to leave the country and abandon his property to outlaws . . . when finally these outlaws fell out among themselves and a war of extermination began. Crime clustered and culminated in murder—a fit ending for the high carnival."

The judge spoke of how United States troops had taken the New Mexican situation in hand, causing large sections of the lawless element to flee the country, then added that the Adjutant General might be interested to know that many of these outlaws, in fact most of them, had moved to Texas to take up headquarters in Pecos, Presidio and El Paso counties.

"I was told while holding court in Pecos," he went on, "that it was the intention of some of these men to settle in the unorganized county of Crockett, in this district, where there are no settlements at present, and which is bordering on the Republic of Mexico. How can civil officers cope with this colony of outlaws, rich in plunder, bold, desperate, daring and skillful, with Mexico as a land of refuge, if there be no state aid?" he asked.

The letter went back as far as 1875 in its statement of atrocities. In that year, it was pointed out, a band of outlaws had brought stolen cattle to Presidio and Pecos county and had offered them for sale. They had terrorized the district. They had visited the stores to take what they wanted. They had even ridden through the streets and the military post at Fort Davis shouting, shooting pistols, and defying officers.

And then in 1877 similar bands had visited the town of Fort Stockton and had shot up stores when owners refused to serve free whiskey. They had even killed pack burros in the street—just to get a little target practice.

"I am well satisfied," concluded Judge Blacker, "that if the legislature does not provide some material aid to the civil authorities in the crime-stricken districts of the frontier that the courts will be closed, that civil law will be suspended, that anarchy and lawlessness will ensue, and that there will be a receding frontier whose boundary will be marked alone by the sword, the pistol, the shotgun and the rifle."

In this sombre portrait of the country he did not, of course, neglect to mention "the recent El Paso county troubles"—which might have been infinitely worse had the affair found recruits among the last instead of the earlier sweepings of the feud which raged across the line.

But even with competition the Salt War of San Elizario did its part in upholding the red tradition of the times.

THE SAN ELIZARIO SALT WAR

CHAPTER ELEVEN

SALT . . .

About ninety miles eastward from the city of El
Paso, on the westward slope of the Guadalupe Mountains and a few miles north of the Sierra Diablo, the
wandering traveler may find a series of waterless little
lakes which furnish ample proof that Mother Nature
often takes great pains to provide her thankless children with the raw necessities of life.

There, like a group of basins set for the feet of the
mountains, nestle the Lakes of Guadalupe, natural
reservoirs containing an abundance of that element
which, since the beginning of time, has been one of the
prime requirements for human existence—Salt.

But don't imagine, if you should come across those
shining gems of white upon the desert, that you have
made a discovery, because for many, many years—even
when Spain and Mexico ruled the country—the salt
deposits were in general use by citizens living on both
sides of the Rio Grande.

A road had been built to the spot and over it for
scores of years had traveled the carts from Mexico
and the Border country, to load and take the ancient
highway home again; for the product of the lakes was
pure enough to use without refinement, and best of
all—it was free.

Even after the Treaty of Guadalupe-Hidalgo and the

107

annexation of Texas by the United States—which, of course, gave Texas title to the property—the salt was free to all who cared to come and take it, whether they lived on the north or the south bank of the Rio Grande. The carts continued to move happily along the ancient highway . . .

But in the middle '70s there came to the city of El Paso one Charles Howard, a lawyer; and since he had a natural inclination in that direction he wasn't long in town before he began to dabble quite extensively in local politics. He played his cards well. Mustering to his cause some of the principal spellbinders of the community, he put himself up as Democratic candidate for district judge and—with the invaluable aid of Senor Louis Cardis, an Italian by birth but a leader among the Mexicans—found himself elected.

Then, with the campaign safely over, Mr. Howard began looking about him for other fields to conquer, and as fate would have it his first-place choice fell on the Lakes of Guadalupe. Here was a fortune to be made and he wondered why some one hadn't thought of it before . . . and so, as an official and a servant of the people, he let it be known that the salt deposits were of the public domain and therefore open to claim. He neglected to state, however, that said claim already had been staked—by none other than Judge Howard himself!

The ambitious lawyer, assisted in this business by an equally ambitious justice of the peace, Gregoria N. Garcia, had introduced to the Border country a brand new type of politics, and the cry which went up was deafening, and ominous. Turned back from what they had long considered a gift direct from Mother Nature, the citizens of Mexican origin were baffled . . . for many of these people were but *peons* unable to pay even the small price per cartload that Howard demanded for the salt.

In all communities, however, there are certain bold men always ready to take the reins of battle in their teeth and put issues to the test. In this instance they were two Mexican gentlemen of San Elizario, who hitched their carts and announced to all and sundry that they were about to hie themselves to the lakes and take, according to ancient custom, the salt of life. Madonia Gandara and Jose Marie Juarez, however, didn't even get started, for Judge Howard and Garcia heard of the project and had them arrested—just on "intentions."

Naturally, the Latin populace fumed. On that September day of 1877 when the arrests occurred, Howard and Garcia were in San Elizario, a town on the river below El Paso, and within a few hours things began to hum. The Mexicans gathered their arms and under the leadership of Visto Salcido and Leon Granillo formed a mob of sixty men, ten of whom came from the Mexican side of the river.

This group stormed the jail, freed Senors Gandara and Juarez, then went after Judge Howard and Mr. Garcia, who might have felt the rope about their necks but for the foresight of the local authorities in arresting the pair and placing them under guard.

Yet even this precaution failed to give the "salt barons" any great measure of security. Hearing of the arrest, the mob returned to the jail and demanded the new prisoners, but before the issue could be forced the priest of the parish, the Reverend Pierre Bourgad, accompanied by Louis Cardis the highly-respected citizen, arrived on the scene. They argued and they pleaded until at last the temper of the mob was cooled. It dispersed, leaving Howard and Garcia to cheat the hangman's noose.

This was something of a magnanimous gesture on the part of Don Louis. He and Judge Howard had been friends politically—but even so, Cardis had been one of the chief protestants when Howard had filed his "location claims" on the salt lake. Still a power among the Mexicans, he advised against violence, but in an adroit way made it plain that he believed the judge was acting illegally.

Now friend Howard, from the safety of the jail, heard this line of argument and although it undoubtedly saved his life, he knew that with Cardis against him something had to be done if his commercial salt plans were not to go wrong. But the Mexicans didn't intend to give him a chance. Since they had the judge in jail they intended to keep him there. He would be released, they told him, only upon one set of conditions—that he would bind himself with good security in the sum of twelve thousand dollars to relinquish all claim to the salinas, and then leave the country, never to return. As for Garcia, the justice of the peace, resignation was set as the price of his freedom.

The judge bit his lip. This was something of a long order. He had a fortune in Guadalupe Lakes and he wanted to keep it—but finally, after conferring with advisors, he decided to accede to conditions and get out. What good, after all, was salt and money to a dead man?

So he sought and found bondsmen, including John G. Atkinson and Charles E. Ellis, the latter a merchant of the town. The customary papers were signed and the judge rode for New Mexico, where he settled down to think things over and study reports faithfully forwarded by one Mr. McBride, his agent at the lakes. Howard, still hopeful, had told McBride to remain on the job.

But in the process of his thinking in the new environment, the judge suddenly remembered a piece of Texas business he had left unfinished. He had neglected to settle his account with Louis Cardis, who, though opposing his enterprise, had saved him from the mob. Therefore he broke his parole, and on October 10 returned to San Elizario.

Don Louis was writing a letter in his shop when Judge Howard entered with a shotgun in his hands. He died that way—sitting at his desk.

The judge mounted his horse and rode hastily again for New Mexico, and just in time—for hell had broken loose along the Border. It was but natural that the Mexicans should consider the slaying of their favorite a blow directed against themselves, and they prepared to take vengeance after the fashion of a hot-blooded race. They armed and rode upon the fast-made trail of Mr. Howard—but the judge had a good horse.

Safe again in New Mexico, His Honor took his ease and read more reports from Salt Agent McBride. The weeks passed, and then Howard received from his employe a letter which informed him that a train of carts was taking salt from his lakes. The matter should have, he thought, the judge's personal attention.

Howard considered. He knew that Major John B. Jones, commander-in-chief of the Texas Rangers, had been in Ysleta and San Elizario investigating past troubles, and that the Major and Father Bourgad had succeeded somewhat in appeasing the wrath of the Mexican populace; but he knew, too, that Jones had instructed Ranger Lieutenant J. B. Tays to keep an eye on the situation and file reports to the capitol in Austin.

The judge decided to return, but before setting out on the journey sent a message to Tays saying that he had to go to San Elizario on business and asking that an escort be sent from Franklin to meet him at Ysleta. The escort, half dozen men from Company C, was arranged for December 12 and Howard started for the rendezvous.

Meanwhile, San Elizario heard of the impending visit . . . and San Elizario had not forgotten the beloved Don Louis. The Mexicans started gathering, not only the reputable citizens of the town but a vicious assortment of outlaws and cut-throats from over the Border, men who saw in the threatening carnival of vengeance a chance for loot and excitement.

Thus was formed a grim reception committee of

about four hundred men, one-third from Mexico, the remainder from El Paso county. They were led by Chico Barella, Desiderio Apodaca, Ramon Sambrano, Leon Granillo, Cisto Salcido, Anatasio Montez and Acaton Porras, all residents of Texas except Montez.

On the morning of the 12th the mob assembled in the streets of the town to await the coming of Judge Howard, and they made no secret of their intention—to kill him. Atkinson and Ellis the bondsmen, and McBride the salt agent, were nervous. They kept to their homes—for they, too, had received threats against their lives. But whatever else may be said of the judge, he was no coward.

He proceeded to Ysleta as planned. The Ranger escort was waiting, but before it could take the road to San Elizario Lieutenant Tays himself, with twelve men behind him, galloped in from Franklin. The Ranger officer explained that after sending out the escort he had received news of the gathering mob. He had heard, too, that a group of Mexicans were patrolling the road from Ysleta in hope of ambushing the party. But concerning the events of the next few hours let Tays tell his own story as he told it in reports made to the Adjutant General:

"We met at Kerber's house about 4 p. m. and Howard got on a horse and rode down to San Elizario in the ranks. The inhabitants of the town had been expecting us and were all out as we passed their houses, but made no further demonstration. We arrived at the quarters about six o'clock (Ranger quarters) and a number of Howard's friends came to see him. He went over to spend the night with C. Ellis, and fearing an outbreak I put a double guard on the quarters.

"All was quiet until about ten o'clock when the watch came in and informed me there was a disturbance in the direction of Leon Granillo's house. I got out, and was informed that some of the men had made a speech and ordered a charge on our quarters."

That wasn't the only cause of the disturbance, though Tays didn't know it yet. Ellis, bondsman and host to Howard, had heard of the meeting at Granillo's house, and after telling the judge he believed he could put an end to the trouble, slipped a revolver in his right boot, and started for the place. He found a gathering of several hundred Mexicans, none apparently in the best of humor.

"What does this mean, *muchachos?*" he demanded. "Don't act foolishly. Let me advise you for your own good . . .

But his remarks were immediately cut short by a shout from Leon Granillo, standing with a group of compatriots in the yard.

"Ahora es tiempo!"

("Now is the time!")

Eutemio Chaves, swinging a lasso, rode up on horseback. Ellis, realizing the import of Granillo's *"ahora es tiempo,"* reached for the gun in his boot, but too late. Even as he stooped the noose settled down about his shoulders and tightened.

Chaves, with a yell, spurred his horse—which reared, then plunged forward into a run, dragging the unfortunate Ellis along behind. For three hundred yards his body bumped over the rough terrain, but mercifully he lost consciousness before the end of that wild ride.

In the edge of a series of sandhills Chaves reined in. He got down, took off his rope, and leaned over the merchant. Something flashed in the starlight, and then Chaves mounted and rode back to the house of Granillo —to join the avalanche of hate and vengeance which was about to sweep down upon the town of San Elizario.

Lieutenant Tays did not know that Ellis had gone to the Granillo house, but after going into the streets and hearing reports on the disturbance, he sensed that serious trouble was on the way. He took immediate steps to strengthen defenses at the 'dobe house and corral, which the Rangers used as headquarters when they chanced to come to San Elizario. But to resume his report:

"In a few minutes they started. We could hear them yelling and giving orders. I placed some men on the roof, some on the opposite building and a few in the corral, and gave orders not to fire until fired on by the mob. They came within one hundred yards of the quarters and then retreated. Howard had come to the quarters at the first noise and had demanded protection. He said that Ellis had started out when the riot commenced and had not returned. This was the last time he was ever seen by his friends. His body was found in the sandhills two days later, his scalp, eyebrows and beard taken, his throat cut from ear to ear, and stabbed twice in the heart.

"The night passed off without further incident, and at daylight I found that our quarters were surrounded by three lines of pickets, who had stretched rawhide ropes across the openings and cut holes to command them in such a manner that it was impossible for us to go out and charge them. At the outside of the lines they had squads of cavalry stationed about 200 yards apart, and numbering about 20 men in each.

"I placed three men on John Clark's house, and John Atkinson went with them. Miguel Garcia (a Ranger previously sent to guard Ellis' store) asked for more men and I sent him his son, G. D., and Frank Kent. Atkinson brought over a trunk containing $700 in specie. Cisto Salcido had told him they would give us three hours to deliver Howard, and if we did not do so they would take him out and shoot him."

And Salcido, that pleasant fellow, had sent still another warning to the Rangers.

"You are interfering with our business." he said. "Give us Howard . . . or we will burn you, too."

The lieutenant refused. The Mexicans closed in—to write in blood the climax of another Texas feud.

Salt, which sustains life, was about to take its toll . . .

CHAPTER TWELVE

. . . AND BLOOD

Before nine o'clock on the morning of December 13 it became plainly apparent to Lieutenant Tays and his Rangers that only a miracle could save them if they persisted in holding Judge Howard from the mob which howled for his blood outside the barricaded 'dobe house.

Tays had but a few more than a score of men, while during the night the ranks of the four hundred attackers had been reinforced by small bands from across the Rio Grande. The *Mexicanos* of the Republic had lived for years in neighborly friendship with the Latin-speaking residents of Texas—the two groups intimately bound together in the bonds of common faith, like sympathies and tastes—and it was only natural that the over-the-river boys should be eager to share the fun attendant on the massacre of the *gringos*.

Things looked none too cheerful for the Rangers and the salt barons. Tays was worried, but determined. He would make every effort to hold the fort, and hope for reinforcements from El Paso.

Howard was silent. He went to the window at intervals to gaze at the crowd . . . proof enough that the salt lakes were slipping from his grasp. But if events did turn as he hoped they would he still intended to go through with the business which had brought

117

him to San Elizario—replevin of salt lately taken from
the deposits by unauthorized persons.

At nine o'clock Tays sent for the three men he had
posted as guard on the nearby home of John Clark,
and with four others he put them on the roof of
Ranger headquarters with orders to fire at the first sign
of attack.

He wondered about the three men stationed in the
Ellis store down the block, and he sent Sergeant C. E.
Mortimer to investigate. Mortimer reached the store in
safety, found the men still holding it, and then proceeded liesurely down the street to get a first-hand view
of conditions. He stopped and turned back but as he
did so a shot rang from the window of a house across
the street.

The sergeant staggered, cried out that he had been
shot, and then started running toward the Ranger quarters as rifles and revolvers began popping from all
directions. The battle of San Elizario was on . . .

Mortimer tried vainly to reach his companions, but
failed. Near the mill, across the way from Ranger
quarters, he fell.

Lieutenant Tays, looking from a window, saw at
once what had occurred and without a word he un-
barred the door, stepped out in the hail of bullets and
rushed to the sergeant's side. He lifted the wounded
man to his shoulders and started back, the Rangers
on the roof covering the rescue. But the heroic deed
was all in vain. Mortimer, shot through the back,
already was dying.

And now the mob pushed in closer to the 'dobe

house, so close that it was impossible for the men on the roof to return their fire. Tays ordered the seven down and with the others they took up positions in the quarters and in the corral, and from that time until four o'clock in the afternoon both sides kept up a sniping engagement which left a dozen Mexicans wounded in the streets.

Let us turn again to the lieutenant's report:

"At this time the justice of the peace came in under a flag of truce and told us that the Mexicans did not want to fight, and that he would be personally responsible for them that night if they fired on us. I sent one of my men to the roof shortly after and the moment he appeared they fired on him from all angles. One ball tore off the top of his hat and another went through his coat. I then barricaded the doors, opened portholes in the windows, and stationed two men in each room and at the doors. The firing almost stopped during the night."

In the dawn the Mexicans charged the corral, but the lead from a dozen Winchesters repulsed the assault with few casualties. Two other attacks were made during the morning, but both were driven back handily. Then Frank Kent slipped out of the Ellis store and made his way to the quarters.

He had an alarming report to make. The Mexicans, he said, had succeeded in entering John Atkinson's home next door and even then were engaged in cutting the connecting wall. They might break through at any moment, but the Garcias still were holding out.

Firing continued throughout the day but as evening

fell the Mexicans completed their tunnel and captured
the store. The Garcias escaped under cover of a Ranger
volley and made their way to the quarters, leaving the
Mexicans to plunder the merchandise. The store was
looted, the windows fortified with sacks of flour, and
with this new breastwork in their possession the Mexicans opened fire with renewed enthusiasm. All through
the night of the 14th and the morning of the 15th the
intermittent sniping went on, with red tongues of flame
spurting from the store—to receive answer from the
portholes of the 'dobe house.

At noon Tays put up a flag. He told the attackers
that the sheriff of Pecos county, who had been with the
party from the first, wanted to go through the lines,
his immediate return home having become imperative.
The Mexicans agreed to let him out, but asked for a
parley with the lieutenant. Tays then met with the
leaders and it was agreed that there should be no firing
during the night and that another conference would
be held in the morning.

The Mexicans kept their word, but erected fortifica-
tions and dug rifle pits during the night—which engi-
neering projects they used as an argument to gain
custody of Judge Howard, who had been doing his
part with a rifle from behind the barricade.

"We have tunneled under your quarters and packed
the place with gunpowder," said the leaders, "and you
will be wise, senors, to surrender Howard. If you do
not . . . then pouf! . . . we shall blow up the house.
All we ask is this . . . that Howard come down to us of

his own free will and promise to relinquish all claim to the salinas."

"And with such a promise," added Chico Barella, chief of the mobsmen, "I swear by the Holy Cross that none of those involved in the salt troubles shall be harmed."

Tays made no answer, but he returned to the adobe house and told Howard what had been offered.

"Then I'll go," said the judge, after a moment's reflection. "It is the only chance to save your lives, though I feel sure they will kill me."

"I am not asking you to go," protested the lieutenant. "If you want to stay my men will protect you to the last . . . you know that."

But Howard was determined.

"Yes, I know," he said, "but it is useless to try and stand them off any longer. This is our only chance to escape, and I'll agree to the conditions . . . take me down."

He shook hands with all the Rangers, thanked them for what they had done, gave all his valuables to Mc-Bride and then like a man resigning himself to fate, left the building with Tays. They met the leaders of the mob in a house across the street, but as it happened there was none in either party who could properly act as interpreter, and so Tays sent word to his quarters for John Atkinson to come over. Atkinson could speak excellent Spanish.

The Mexicans immediately took the Howard bondsman to another room for a conference, leaving the Ranger and Howard under guard in an adjoining chamber. Shortly Atkinson came out. He told Tays that all would be settled, but that he must first go to the quarters for McBride. In a few minutes he returned, not only with McBride, but with the entire Ranger company! And while the surprised lieutenant watched from another room the Mexicans disarmed the entire group. Then Tays was told that he could join his men . . . to learn for the first time that they had surrendered: that they had come across the street to the enemy on representations by Atkinson that all had been arranged, and that Tays desired the surrender. Of course Tays raised a merry row, but the deed was done.

John Atkinson, to save his own life, had betrayed the Texas Rangers—and had paid into the bargain eleven thousand dollars in specie!

But Howard, Atkinson and McBride were not yet out of the fire. Chico Barella had taken an oath on the Cross that harm should not come to the three, but now—as the Mexicans met in secret conclave—a messenger had arrived from over the Border. He carried a note from a priest of the church and on it was scribbled these words:

"Kill all the *gringos*. I will absolve you."

Chico smiled to himself . . . and thirty minutes later Howard, Atkinson and McBride were informed that they had been sentenced to death.

The mob at San Elizario made short work of the business. As one eye-witness described it in an affidavit made later to state officials:

Howard was taken out first, and with the mob

formed into a regiment about six hundred strong, marched to the place of execution. He walked erectly with his hands behind him, and when the spot was reached and the command "halt!" given, he stopped instantly and turned to face his executioners.

All was as silent as death. Then Desiderio Apodaca, with a firing party of eight men, came up and took positions about ten feet from the doomed man, who stood quietly watching the proceedings. When all was ready Howard spoke. He was not fluent in Spanish but he managed to make himself understood.

"You are about to execute three hundred men," he said, though none of the witnesses knew exactly what he meant.

Then he bared his chest and gave the word himself —"Fire!"

The squad pressed down on the triggers and the "salt baron" of Guadalupe fell kicking and squirming on the ground.

Jesus Telles, one of the mobsmen, then ran to the spot and raising a *machete* in both hands, struck at the body. The blow fell, but Howard, in his death throes, turned . . . and the blow descended on Telles' own left foot, chopping off two of his toes.

The crowd then hacked the body to ribbons, dragged it to an old well and threw it in. Never again would Charles Howard stop a salt cart on its way to the Lakes of Guadalupe . . .

John Atkinson, when his turn came, could not understand. He appeared, at first, a little dazed by the turn events had taken.

"Do you intend to violate your pledge?" he asked the mob leaders as he and McBride were led before the firing party.

A roar from the crowd was his answer.

"Acabenlos!"

("Finish them!")

"There is no remedy?" asked Atkinson.

"No!" shouted the crowd, in chorus.

"Then let me die with honor," said the man whose crime was furnishing unpaid bail for Charles Howard. "I will give the word."

He took off his coat and vest, unbuttoned his shirt to bare his chest, looked up at his eight executioners and gave his final order:

"When I give the word fire at my heart . . . Fire!"

Eight rifles popped, eight bullets struck the condemned man in the stomach, but still he kept his feet. He staggered, recovered himself, and gazed defiantly at the firing squad.

"Mas arriba, carbrones!" he shouted. "Higher up, you——!"

Two more shots were fired and Atkinson toppled to the ground.

But still he was not dead!

He turned his head slightly, gazed at Desiderio Apodaca, and with one last feeble gesture pointed to his own temple.

Apodaca drew his pistol, stepped up and gave the requested *coup de grace*.

McBride the salt agent profited from the rifle practice which had gone before. He died instantly, and his body was dragged away with that of Atkinson.

The great salt feud of San Elizario was over . . .

In days which followed the officers of El Paso county went out after the mob leaders. They killed several, including Telles the toe-chopper, and during the cleanup work the deputies and the state Rangers were accused of shooting down many persons innocent of complicity in the executions . . . while most of the real culprits hid in Mexico.

On February 3, 1878, Allen Blacker, judge of the Twentieth Judicial District, arrived in El Paso from Tom Green county to conduct an investigation, and on the following day had an interview with the *jefe politico* in Juarez across the international line.

He asked for the arrest of all Mexican citizens of Texas, participants in the mob, who were then taking refuge in Mexico. The *jefe politico* was very cordial. He displayed an order from the governor of Chihuahua calling for apprehension of the suspects and return of all property purloined during that hectic three-day fight.

But strange to say, few arrests ever were made, and little property accounted for. Somehow, from the Mexican point-of-view, the whole affair now seemed rather unimportant.

They only knew that the little carts were running again along the ancient road which led to the Lakes of Guadalupe.

. . . Salt, in the business of life, is a vital and important thing . . .

RIFLES IN THE DUSK

John Pinkney Calhoun Higgins, and the leaders in his faction. *Top row, left to right*: Powell Woods, second unknown; Buck Allen, A. T. Mitchell, one of the last survivors of the fight on courthouse square. *Lower row, left to right*: Felix Castello, Jess Standard, Bob Mitchell, and Pink Higgins.

—Photo courtesy Standard Studio, Lampasas.

CHAPTER THIRTEEN

THE HORRELL-HIGGINS AFFAIR

On a March evening in the year of grace 1873 the good citizens of Lampasas held a mass meeting to consider the state of the county, and if in conclusion they accomplished little else the participants went home with one thought uppermost in mind—that the state of the county wasn't much to boast about.

The meeting really was just a supplement to another. Earlier in the day there had been a smaller but vastly more important gathering at which a group of serious-faced gentlemen had set themselves down to write the following words upon a form provided for the purpose:

"We, the inquest jury, from the evidence before us, find that Captain Thomas Williams, Wesley Cherry and J. M. Daniels came to their deaths by pistol and gun shots in the Lampasas Saloon, in the town of Lampasas, in the state of Texas, on Friday the fourteenth of March, 1873, from and by the hands of Thomas Horrel, Martin Horrel, Merrett Horrel, et al, etc. . . ."

Followed then the signatures of the various jurors, together with the seal and certification of one Mr. Thomas Pratt, justice of the peace and acting coroner . . . all of which might seem to indicate that a fracas

of some proportions had occurred in the town during
the day.

Such, indeed, was the case. Three men were dead
and the fourth was dying—but considering time and
place even this wholesale killing might not have elicited
much concern had it not been for the fact that the
victims were state policemen. That was the principal
reason for the meeting, but there were other things to
consider, too.

Affairs in Lampasas had been bad for a long while.
The cattle gentry of the community had certain play-
ful habits which were tending to keep the more peace-
loving residents of the town in a continual state of
nervousness. Of late they were finding particular pleasure in riding through the streets shooting with revolvers
at knot-holes in the fronts of the boarded buildings,
and as a result some of the structures were perforated
with as many as fifty bullet holes.

Even the editor of the weekly *Dispatch,* who had
noted in his columns some of the wilder events of the
day, lately had abandoned all hope of sitting behind
glass windows, for the "boys" shot out the panes faster
than he could have them replaced. Things had, in
truth, reached such a pass that one warning yell for the
citizens to "hide out" was quite enough to cause a
general locking of doors and a hurried barring of
windows.

And in all this atmosphere of western jollity none
played a greater part than the brothers Horrel . . . Tom,
Merrett, Sam, Bert, Ben and Bill. Sons of old Samuel
Horrel, they were good boys . . . or had been . . . and

they came from one of the best and most highly re-
spected families in that section of the state; but like
all cattlemen of that day and time they liked sometimes
to refresh themselves at the local bars . . . and bars
in the '70s were not places where one was apt to avoid
trouble. The Horrels were not long in finding their full
share, as witness the incident on the morning of
March 14th . . .

Captain Williams, with Privates Cherry, Daniels,
Melville and four others, had arrived in Lampasas at
the request of certain citizens who wanted to see if
something could be done to remedy the aforementioned
conditions prevailing at the time

The detachment, part of the state force recruited by
Edmund J. Davis, the carpet-bagger governor, scarcely
had hitched their horses in front of the Lampasas
saloon, on the west side of the square, before one of
the habitues of the place swaggered from the doorway
with a Colt revolver strapped about his waist.

"Wait a minute, Bill," said Captain Williams, who
knew the man. "Aren't you forgetting something? You
know as well as I do there's a state law now against
totin' six-shooters in the streets. I'll have to put you
under arrest."

The man surrendered meekly, handed over his Colt,
and then politely asked the captain if he might return
to the saloon for a word with a friend before going
to jail.

"Sure," said Williams, "and I'll go with you."

These were the last words, perhaps, that Williams
of the State Police ever uttered—for as he entered

with his prisoner he was greeted by a barrage of Winchester fire from across the bar and from behind the tables. The captain never knew what struck him. He dropped dead in the doorway—two bullets through his body and one through his head.

Hearing the firing within, Privates Cherry and Daniels drew their revolvers and rushed the doorway . . . but they were expected. Riddled with carbine slugs, they died beside the body of their officer.

Outside, the remaining policemen cocked back the hammers of their guns and waited, for they knew that sooner or later somebody would be making an exit from that saloon, either their fellow-officers or the enemy. And they were right. The wild bunch came— their guns blazing.

In the first volley Private Melville went down with a mortal wound in the lungs, but before he fell he got in one shot, which scratched Thomas Horrel. The other officers, meantime, had opened fire and after a brief exchange the Horrels retired to the saloon, leaving the troopers to carry away their dying comrade. The one negro member of the police force already had mounted his horse and fled.

The Horrels themselves didn't tarry long upon the scene of conflict. With their friends they took up their reins, vaulted into the saddles, and took to the woods —while the surviving state officers got off messages to Austin asking Governor Davis to send down reinforcements as soon as possible. Davis acted at once. He advised Adjutant General F. L. Britton to visit the scene in person; and next day Britton, with a party of ten men, arrived in Lampasas. He found plenty of help on hand. Even before his arrival two Minute Men companies had mobilized—the Lampasas county group under Lieutenant Lee, and the Burnet county organization under Sergeant W. H. Shelburne. In addition Sheriff S. T. Denson had formed a small posse.

These forces combined for a five-day scout over Lampasas, Burnet, Coryell, Williamson and Llano counties, and they caught two men—Mart Horrel and Jerry Scott the saloon keeper—whom they lodged in jail at Georgetown before breaking up to return home.

But the pair didn't remain long in the Williamson county bastile. Late one night while the town lay asleep a party of men slipped up to the jail, used a heavy sledge hammer on the door, and invited Horrel and Scott to step out into the wide open spaces. Needless to say, they went . . . and within a few days the Horrels and their friends mustered, rode for Lampasas, where the boys gathered up their cattle and personal belongings, and took the long and dusty trail for New Mexico . . . a territory then considered suitable sanctuary for those seeking to avoid the long reach of the law.

They settled near Ruidoso, but they hadn't been long in their new home before they found themselves involved in new difficulties.

It all started when Bill Horrel, visiting the town, dropped in on a fandango near San Juan church. During the evening he argued with a *caballero* of the Latin blood, and when the commotion raised by the ensuing fight had quieted sufficiently to determine the status of the two contestants, Bill lay slashed and bleeding

on the floor, the Mexican standing over him with a
red-stained knife in his right hand.

The slain man's brothers and their friends heard of
the affair scarcely before it was over and lost no time
in getting to the spot . . . and before they rode from
town again the score not only had been settled five
times over, but there had been a fight in which one
sheriff, a deputy, and a constable had been left wallow-
ing in the dust.

The matter, however, didn't end there. Scrap after
scrap followed and in one of them Ben Horrel was
killed, thus opening the way for a racial feud during
which upward of half a hundred Mexicans along the
Hondo were made useless for the purpose of future
fandangoes.

After a time, however, the boys grew tired of this
rather monotonous fray and they decided to go back to
Texas. They returned to Lampasas and upon the advice
of friends, who assured them a fair trial, they surrendered to face a jury in connection with the killing
of Williams. Sentiment against the carpet-bagger governor and his state police had been running rather
high, and so after a brief hearing all the Horrels
charged in the saloon affair were acquitted.

They settled down to peaceful ways—but not for
long.

Enter now John Pinkney Calhoun Higgins on the
scene.

Pink Higgins, as he was more familiarly known in
the Lampasas country, was of a neighboring family,
the son of John H. Higgins, a Georgian who had

brought his family to Texas in 1848 and had moved into the Lampasas area from Austin in the early months of 1857.

Old John had settled down within a few miles of the Horrel homestead and since the two families had been forced to share alike the perils and the hardships of the frontier, they had been on the most friendly terms. Old John had been known to remark on more than one occasion that Samuel Horrel, head of the clan which bore his name, was without doubt "one of the best neighbors a man ever had"—and Samuel, in his turn had often seen fit to return the compliment.

Even the lads had been good friends in the days of their boyhood, but if something had occurred to change the Horrel boys during their stay in New Mexico, something also had happened to Pink during their absence.

Pink was now a grown man, a strapping big fellow who was putting to good advantage the lessons learned with the rifle and the revolver in the days of his youth . . . when he had helped his father fight off Indians who prowled about their home. He had risen in the world. He was a high-ranking officer in the post-bellum Ku Klux Klan movement in that part of the state, but at this time he was making his living in cattle—collecting and driving Lampasas herds up the trail to Kansas markets. His education was limited to the cow camps, the horse corrals and the trails. He possessed a cool demeanor, a steady eye, and a hand quick on the draw, and having proved this latter accomplishment on more than one occasion, the people roundabout had learned that he was not a man to trifle with. So much for Pink . . .

The Horrel boys, having established slaughter pens in the country and a meat market in the town, found themselves, shortly after their return to Texas, involved in a quarrel with young Higgins. It all came about through a misunderstanding over some steers and one word led to another until Merrett Horrel and Pink both had made plain the information that they might be expected to open fire on sight.

And then they met—in that same saloon where Captain Williams had found death. Pink had come to town with a friend, Bob Mitchell, and while visiting in a hardware store was apprised of certain remarks Merrett Horrel was alleged to have made earlier in the day.

Higgins, his anger aroused, examined his gun to see that it was ready for use, strode across the square and entered the Lampasas Saloon, his trigger finger already crooked and ready.

Horrel was sitting in a chair, a Winchester rifle across his lap, and as Higgins walked through the doorway he knew instinctively that affairs had reached the showdown—but instead of picking up the Winchester and using it, as might have been expected, Horrel reached for his pistol holster.

To make a long story short, Higgins pulled the trigger first . . . and Horrel slumped from the chair, a few feet from the spot where Captain Williams had died before him.

The saloon emptied within a few seconds, the friends

of the deceased mounting to ride south and inform
Tom Horrel what had happened to his brother; Higgins and Mitchell to mount their respective horses and
take the road for home.

The first party, however, must have ridden fast, for
Higgins and Bob Mitchell were but a few miles out
of town when they met Tom galloping toward
Lampasas. He was armed with a Winchester and a
pistol, and a meeting was not to be avoided; but
trouble on this occasion was averted when Tom threw
away his Winchester and Mitchell dissuaded Pink from
taking summary action. They all rode on . . .

The shooting in Lampasas saloon, however, proved
only the prelude to another, and a worse affair. Pink
remained away from the town for a few days and then,
learning that a murder charge had been filed against
him, grouped his friends about him and started for
Lampasas to put up bond. The day was June 7, 1877.

The party entered on Liveoak street, which cuts into
the Square at the northwest corner, and Higgins, as
he rode in, was accompanied by three friends. They
rode two and two—Bob Mitchell and W. R. Wren in
front, Pink and B. F. Terry, a brother-in-law, behind.

They lolled in the saddles in the fashion of leisurely
cowmen, but they kept their eyes about them, watching
carefully every movement along the street. And then,
a block from the intersection which marked the corner
of the Square, it happened—a sudden roar and the
swishing drive of a lump of lead.

Tom Horrel, seeing his enemy approach, had entrenched himself in the doorway of a building on the corner and had opened up with a pistol.

Pink Higgins wheeled his horse, dug in his spurs and started on a run for help, for he knew that a score of his sympathizers were assembled even then at a point four miles away.

The other three piled off their mounts to seek cover behind the nearby buildings, and all reached safety unscathed save Bill Wren, lately a sheriff of the county. He was slightly wounded in the hip by a bullet from Tom Horrell's gun.

The men had jerked their Winchesters free of their saddle scabbards as they sought cover, and now Bob Mitchell, a kinsman of Pink squatted down behind a pile of stone and prepared himself to take Tom Horrel's measure.

Horrel didn't make a very good target but the few trial shots that Mitchell put over came so close that Tom's eyes were filled with dust. His style cramped in this manner, he retreated to seek another sanctuary around the building corner.

Meanwhile, other warriors had been rushing to the scene of conflict and now the firing had become general, with ten or twelve men on each side.

Up a side street west of the Square were three other members of the Mitchell family—Frank and Alonzo, brothers of Bob, and their father, Mac. Frank and his father were at a store unloading flour from a wagon and as the Horrel sympathizers began to join in the firing Frank was in the act of lifting a sack of flour from the wagon. He was just entering the store with his burden when a bullet, fired from an alley across the street, took him in the back.

He dropped dead just inside the store, whereupon Henry Yates, a bystander and a friend of Frank Mitchell, jerked his revolver, ran to the door, and winged the retreating slayer, a man whose identity has been lost in the silence maintained by the participants since that hectic day.

A. L. Mitchell, seeing his brother fall, ran across the street, borrowed a Sharps rifle, then stationed himself in the second story of a building on the corner to pot-shoot any of the opposition faction that might venture within his range—but the Horrels and their friends had by this time entrenched themselves pretty well in store buildings and behind the masonry of a building being erected on the Square.

Here they remained, answering shot for shot the sniping fire of Bob Mitchell, Wren and Terry, until Pink returned to the scene of combat with reinforcements. He brought with him about thirty-five men, and for thirty minutes or more they made life a merry affair for the Horrel party, grown now to a total strength of about fifteen.

Already three or four men lay dead in the streets, and more might have gone to join them but for the interference of Captain John Sparks of the Rangers, who happened to be in Lampsas with four men. Sparks got to the leaders, persuaded them to cease firing, and then took a section of the Horrel faction in charge, placing them under guard in a building on the corner of the square.

The Ranger captain prevailed on the Higgins-
Mitchell group to go home, and then released the Horrels. In the light of modern viewpoint this may appear
rather strange, but it must be remembered that in the
Seventies men's actions were based on different stand-
ards and different codes . . . and who was Sparks to
say whether the Horrels or the Higgins were to blame
in the family affair?

Anyhow, he allowed both sides to go their way in
peace, and then he filed reports to Austin . . . a report
which was followed swiftly by the arrival of a Ranger
detachment under Captain N. O. Reynolds, accompanied by the commander-in-chief of the state force,
Major John B. Jones himself. The Major, undoubtedly,
was one of the busiest men in Texas during the '70s.

Although the opposing factions met in one or two
unimportant brushes before the arrival of the Rangers,
Major Jones made it plain at once that he intended to
seek a settlement, if possible, without many arrests,
but since the Horrels didn't seem inclined to come in
for a palaver he sent Captain Reynolds and a detachment to find them. And it was on this occasion that
Reynolds displayed the bravery that has immortalized
him forever on the rolls of the Rangers.

Leaving Lampasas with four men of his command
and accompanied by three of the Higgins faction, Bob
Mitchell, Bill Wren and A. L. Mitchell, the captain
set out through an evening drizzle with the Horrel
home on Sulphur Fork as destination.

Approaching the place the party of eight stopped
on a hill above the farm and after Bob Mitchell had

pointed out the house, Reynolds told his men that the entire party would wait there until the early hours of morning, and then make the arrests.

Through the long hours of the night they waited in the rain and then, about four o'clock in the morning, the captain ordered an advance.

Silently the eight men crept toward the house. A few yards away they halted and waited and then, since nothing occurred to hint that their approach had been noticed, they advanced to the door.

Here Reynolds hesitated for a moment. He knew that in all probability the two remaining Horrels, Tom and Mart, were lying asleep surrounded by half a dozen or more of their followers—but he hesitated only for a moment. Whispering to his men to wait outside, he gently pushed open the door and entered, his Winchester ready.

Treading like a cat, he gained the center of the room, and as his eyes grew accustomed to the darkness he made out the forms of six or eight men sprawled about the chamber on beds and pallets.

Reynolds trained his rifle on one of the beds, the one he believed to be the resting place of the Horrel brothers, and then—

"Wake up, boys," he ordered.

The entire group gained consciousness immediately and one of the men on the bed moved as though to reach for a weapon.

Reynolds lowered the muzzle of his gun and pressed the trigger, just as a warning gesture to prove he meant business, but the shot set fire to the bedclothes and mattress.

The waiting Rangers entered—to find the Horrels and their comrades fighting flames.

Some bond making took place in Lampasas that day, with both sides putting up the collateral; and from that time on the Horrel-Higgins affair, as a feud, was over.

Now, only two of the Horrels were left, Sam already having departed from the district, but these two—Tom and Mart—were doomed to a worse fate than death before the guns of a family enemy.

An old man named Vaughn, keeper of a store at Meridian, in a county to the north, was robbed and slain. Whether the Horrel brothers did it or not no man can say with any degree of certainty, but on the testimony of a blacksmith who swore that horse tracks leading from the scene of the crime were made by a peculiar set of horse shoes he had made for one of the brothers who had brought in his mount to be shod, Tom and Mart were arrested and locked in the Meridian jail.

On a Sunday night shortly thereafter the jailor received an urgent message asking him to come home at once—that a member of his family was dying. The good man had no sooner left his post than a large band of men appeared in the vicinity. The visitors first went to a nearby church where a meeting was being held, told the congregation to continue their singing and then, after locking the doors of the meeting house, moved toward the jail.

It took the mob but a few minutes to gain access to the place, and once inside they sought out the cell of Mart and Tom Horrel. One of the boys—records do not reveal which—wanted to pray; but the other stepped forth bravely with the remark: "If I've got to take it, let me have it."

The mobsmen did, while a trembling negro prisoner held high a coal oil lamp which cast grotesque and dancing shadows on the walls.

The jailor, returning later, found the two bodies . . . and enough buckshot on the floor to fill the crown of a good-sized hat. Thus died the last of the Horrel brothers . . . and a bitter family feud.

What of Pink Higgins? He later drifted north to Kent county—to take a "protection" job on the great Spur Ranch, at that time a cattle kingdom covering six hundred and seventy-three thousand acres of the southern Panhandle.

It was a job for which Pink was admirably fitted. Cattle stealing was rife in those days and the Spur wanted Pink to ride the range and put to death, in any manner that he might see fit, any chance cow thieves he might come across. The great ranch had a "protection fund" set aside for that very purpose.

Higgins did his work well—so well, indeed, that ere the day of his retirement he had earned the right to place from fourteen to eighteen notches on the handle of his gun . . . which, of course, he didn't do.

But had he been of the fictional type of gun slinger one notch, perhaps, might have been a little deeper

than the rest—the one representing Mr. Bill Standifer,
his co-partner on that Spur "protection" job.

Yes, Pink got him, too. You see, it was this way—
Pink and Bill both had come from Lampasas county,
and in the early days Bill, if not directly allied with
the opposition faction, had given it his sympathy.
Naturally, bad blood arose between the two, and one
day Pink heard that Bill was planning to get the drop
and shoot him down.

Higgins tried to avoid the issue. He kept indoors
for a time to avoid Standifer until, as he put it himself, he was "tired of being holed up like a rat."

Then he rode out one morning to meet his enemy.
The two men came together on the range, both riding
in the same direction in a manner which made it inevitable that their trails would converge.

Later Pink told the story to Charles A. Jones, one-
time manager of the Spur. He used these words:

"He was on my right and I was sure he would not
get off his horse on my side, but would try to use his
horse as protection. So I made up my mind to keep
my eye on his left foot, and the minute that foot left
the stirrup I would get off and go for my gun.

"We were less than a hundred yards apart and getting closer every step. He slipped her out, and off I
went. My rifle sorter hung in the saddle scabbard, and
as I got it out Standifer shot, hitting old Sandy, my
horse. Sandy jumped against me and made me shoot
wild . . . and I always hated to lose the first shot.

"Standifer was shooting, but he was jumping around

like a Comanche and his shots were going wild. He was sideways to me, and so thin I knew I had to shoot mighty accurate to get him. I knew he couldn't do any good with his gun till he stopped jumping. So I dropped on my knee, trying to get a bead on him, and when he slowed down I let him have it.

"I knew I had got him when the dust flew out of his sleeve above the elbow and he started to buckle. He dropped the gun into the crook of his arm and tried to walk off. I called to him, saying if he had had enough I wouldn't shoot again and would come to him, but he fell face forwards, his feet flopped up, and he didn't speak.

"I was afraid to go to him fearing he was playing possum, so I got on my horse and rode to a telephone and told the sheriff at Claremont I thought I had killed Standifer. He said if I wasn't sure I'd better go back and finish him."

Jones, who pays high tribute to Pink in his memoirs, says that Higgins was one man who had no qualms when it came to talking about his killings, and that he once heard Higgins admit having been indicted in connection with fourteen slayings.

"I didn't kill them all," Pink used to say, "but then I got some that wasn't on the bill . . . so I guess it just about evens up."

The former Lampasas feudsman retired on the Spur "protection fund" and set himself up on a little plot of ground near the ranch. Near Christmas time in 1913 he dropped dead while leaning over his own hearth to light a fire. The heart which had carried him through so many battles had failed him. . . .

* * *

Down in Lampasas not so long ago a reunion was held for all citizens who had been in the county for more than fifty years, and when the picnic feast was set the few surviving relatives of the Horrels broke bread with members of the Higgins and the Mitchell clan. Two daughters of one of the Horrel boys still live in the county . . . and for twelve years, until recently, J. Tom Higgins, son of Pink, was the county judge.

But the judge refuses to talk about the case.

"I have been trying my native best to have those two fine women forget the matter, and if I had my choice I had rather have their votes than all the others in the county. Let the dead past bury its dead," says he.

And that's the way A. T. Mitchell feels about it, too . . . even though he did take a major part in that brawling fight on courthouse square.

Chapter Fourteen

THE MASON COUNTY WAR

There was once a time in Texas when the charge of cattle theft was a weapon just as handy and just as deadly as the pistol and the rifle . . . and if Sheriff John Clark of Mason had not seen fit, in the early days of 1875, to take action against a little group of men he might have escaped a leading role in one of the state's most bloody feuds.

But Sheriff Clark went ahead, and Mason county was plunged into a war of extermination which ended only after the pistol, the shotgun and the hangman's noose had taken heavy toll among the citizenry.

History does not say who first cast the eye of suspicion on Lige Baccus and his cousin, who lived in Loyal Valley—and no man can say until today whether they were guilty of the charge—but history is definite on the fact that the sheriff did go to Loyal Valley with a warrant in his pocket, bring back the pair and lock them in the jail with three companions.

The five, however, were not destined to remain there long. The sheriff, as soon as he had his prisoners comfortably settled, broadcast news of the event; and since there had been a recent epidemic of cattle stealing the citizens of Mason . . . mostly stolid, frugal German settlers . . . decided to make an example of the case in hand.

147

Hence, without stopping to consider whether Baccus and his group might be innocent or guilty, a mob formed near the town, marched on the jail, and announced its intention of taking the five from the custody of the law.

Sheriff Clark had suspected that something of the kind was in the air, and when the mob began forming in the dusk he realized that he must move fast if he was to make even a pretense of saving the group he held behind the bars. He remembered that earlier in the day Captain Dan W. Roberts of the Texas Rangers had come to town to buy grain for the horses of his command, then encamped on the San Saba a few miles north of the town, and so the sheriff hurried to Major Jim Hunter's hotel to confer with the state officer.

Captain Roberts was asleep but Sheriff Clark roused him out, explained the situation, and asked his help. The Ranger dressed as rapidly as possible, strapped on his six-shooter belt, and together the two hurried toward the courthouse.

They found the mob already at the jail door and some of the members, seeing Roberts and Clark approach, warned them to keep back.

"We won't hurt you if you keep your distance," they said, "but don't try to stop us . . . we're going to have these men."

The officers saw at once that it was useless to argue, and so they backed away to the courthouse entrance, slipped inside, and rushed upstairs to the second floor. Then Clark took a Winchester from his office and trained it out a window.

"Keep away from that jail door!" he shouted at the crowd below. "I'll kill the first damn man who touches it! Stand back!"

The mob obeyed. Not a man moved, and for a time it appeared that the sheriff might be able to put over the bluff . . . but Clark didn't know what the mobsmen knew. Even then some of its members were slipping into the courthouse to force the issue.

Captain Roberts and a companion, James Trainer, started down the stairs to watch the door, but they met the mobsmen coming up. The group, numbering about ten, pushed past the officers, rushed to the second floor, and trapped Clark without the slightest difficulty. Then the three were escorted from the building and again warned to keep clear.

The sheriff left Roberts and Trainer to keep watch on the crowd and went to muster help, but when he returned a short time later with half a dozen volunteers, he was too late. The mob already had broken down the jail door and had taken out the five prisoners—Baccus, his cousin, and three employes, Tom Turley, a man named Johnson, and a cow hand lately arrived in the country.

The "neck-tie" party was held at a tree a short distance outside the town, but it wasn't by any means a complete success, for the rescue posse came too close behind. In fact the mob had succeeded in swinging only three of their men—the Baccus pair and Turley—before the affair was interrupted.

Following on foot, the sheriff's men spotted the group in the darkness and opened fire at long range.

The lynchers, seeing need for hasty retreat, turned their guns on the newly-arrived cattle puncher, blew out his brains, and then started firing at Johnson.

This lucky fellow, however, had taken advantage of the first excitement to slip the noose from about his neck, and he scrambled over a rail fence to make a get-away. Although he was made target for a veritable hail of bullets he succeeded, in some miraculous manner, in making his escape.

Roberts, Clark and company lost no time in cutting down the three already hanging from the limb, and their quick action saved a life. Turley merely was strangled, and a dash of water from a nearby stream served to revive him . . . although he was so terrified and his neck so swollen that it was several days before he could speak in any intelligent manner.

Johnson, the man who slipped the noose, appeared late next day at the Ranger camp and asked for protection. The captain put him under his own recognizance and ordered him to wait around for the pending grand jury investigation—but before this event could take place Johnson shot a member of the mob, a wheelwright, and made his disappearance.

Naturally, a great deal of excitement was aroused as a result of the lynching, but then something occurred which definitely brought about the formation of two factions—the German cattle families of Mason against the cattlemen of the outlying districts. . .

Tim Williamson was known as a good man. As an employe of Charles Lemberg he was engaged at the time in driving trail herds up to Kansas, and one morning while Williamson was shaping up a herd to take the northern trek he received a visitor.

It was Deputy Sheriff John Worley, and Worley had in his pocket a warrant for Tim's arrest on a charge of cattle theft. It would seem, according to the complaint, that a yearling with the wrong brand had for some reason become mixed in the trail herd.

Lemberg, not wishing to delay the start north, offered to make bond on the spot for his employe but Worley said that arrangements of that sort must be made in Mason, and so the three mounted and set off for town. They hadn't gone far, however, before they noticed a sizeable party of men approaching across the prairie. They came at a gallop, and Tim knew at once what this meant—the Mason mob—and he cast more than one worried glance back over his shoulder.

The three dug in their spurs and rode like the wind across the brown West Texas plain . . . as though the devil himself might be galloping on the trail behind . . . but the posse slowly closed up the distance.

Williamson turned to the deputy.

"Give me my gun," he pleaded, "and let me make a run. I can get away . . . by myself . . . and if I don't that mob'll catch us sure.

"Can't do it, Tim," said Worley, "You're under arrest and I ain't aimin' to let you go."

"And I ain't aimin' to die!" shouted Williamson, urging his horse to greater speed. "I ain't if I can help it."

And then the crack of a gun and the song of a bullet, followed by a dull thud as the lump of lead tore into the shoulder of the horse that Tim was riding. The animal weaved, staggered, and then plunged on again—to cover a full mile before he stumbled and crashed to the ground in a lifeless heap.

Williamson threw himself clear and hit the ground, but the possemen already were riding in with their revolvers drawn. They made short work of Mr. Williamson . . . and then left him dying beside the carcass of his horse.

Worley rode home and thought little more about the matter. And here he made a sad mistake, for Tim had many friends, one in particular—a former Texas Ranger whose reputation in the county already was such that most men had learned to give him a wide berth when they met him on the road. Scott Cooley wasn't exactly a bad actor; he wasn't exactly a criminal or anything like that—he just wasn't the sort of man who took unto his bosom many friends.

Williamson, however, was one of the favored few, and when Scott heard the details concerning his death he swore vengeance, just as did several others among Tim's friends down south in Loyal Valley. George Gladden was one; John Ringgold another; and then there were the Beard brothers, Mose and John. The latter two were Blanco county men but were counted among the best friends of the slain man. Mose was in Loyal Valley at the time visiting in the home of Gladden.

This little group of self-appointed avengers went to work at once, and between them they managed to compile a list of Mason Germans who might have been involved in either the hanging affair or the shooting of

Tim; but before they could strike, the sheriff and a posse—including many of the Germans—met with Mose Beard and Gladden at Keller's store on the Llano river fifteen miles south of Mason.

It is not certain how the shooting started. It was a brief affair, but when it was over Gladden was wounded in the face. Beard, however, was unhurt. He managed to get Gladden on a horse and ride away with him toward Beaver Creek, but on the banks of that stream the wounded man became too weak to travel. So Beard took him from the horse, hid him under a pile of brush and then set out to find a wagon. But before he could leave the vicinity the posse was upon him.

Beard was killed without ceremony, before he had time to make protest, and then the sheriff's men started a search for Gladden. They found him at last under the pile of brush, and one of the possemen, pointing to the wounded man's own gun, suggested:

"Let's finish him with that."

But Charlie Keller, who had joined the party at the store, protested.

"I was raised with him," he said, throwing himself across Gladden, "and I can't stand to see it done."

The posse, after some argument, finally agreed to let the count stand as it was, and that evening Gladden was loaded on a mail hack and sent home to Loyal Valley.

It must have been an uncomfortable ride, but despite his wound the man who traveled parcel post that night —a bloody package on the back seat of the hack—did not die. He lived to help even scores for Mose Beard,

Williamson and the Baccus cousins. He sent to Blanco for Mose's brother John, who came with a shotgun and posted himself over Gladden's bed until the injured man was able to be about.

There followed in the city of Mason a reign of terror too lengthy for recitation here. It is possible that many of the Germans, even leaders like Daniel Hoerster, were led into the feud at the outset by the influence of persons who had grudges to settle, but whatever the case the controversy now had grown to such proportions that few Germans retired at night without a pistol under the pillow.

None knew what might occur next. Men were fired on from ambush; residents were called to their doors and shot.

The killing of a citizen by the name of Cheney was typical of this phase in the fighting. In Moran's Saloon Mr. Cheney had dropped the chance remark that certain citizens of Mason had offered him two thousand dollars to shoot Scott Cooley, who at that time was credited with some of the major offenses in the town.

Moran had warned Cheney, a newcomer, that he had best mind his own business and keep clear of the entire matter, but the warning came too late. Only a few nights later a group of men rode up to Cheney's home and announced themselves with a loud "Hello!"

Cheney opened his door. In the darkness outside (Mason was an unlighted town in those terrible days) he could discern several figures in the yard. The householder asked who called and what was wanted.

"Let's take him along with us," he heard one of the shadows say.

"Oh, why go to that trouble," replied another, impatiently. "Let's get it over with."

There was a roar in the darkness and a spurtle of flame. Cheney dropped in his own doorway, killed by a single shot from a Winchester. John Ringgold later was indicted for the killing.

Meanwhile, George Gladden's wounds had completely healed. He waited until he thought the time auspicious and then, with John Beard and a friend riding beside him, entered Mason one night to settle the score for the slain Mose.

The three men loitered for awhile outside a saloon and just as dusk was falling they saw Sheriff Clark and a group of his friends come riding into town.

"Who's the man riding beside Clark?" asked Beard of a bystander, but the bystander couldn't tell him.

"Well, he may be an innocent man," said Beard, "and I'd rather let the sheriff get away than kill the wrong man. But I do know Dan Hoerster . . . I'll take care of him."

He raised his shotgun to his shoulder.

Hoerster, a leading merchant of the town, was riding behind Clark, and wide enough from the party that he could easily be singled out.

John Beard squinted along the sights and then let go with the right hand barrel. Hoerster toppled from his horse and fell in the street, dead.

Beard and his companions made a run for it and got away with their lives, although Gladden did lose a finger

when a rifle ball, fired by one of a group of snipers in
Major Hunt's hotel, struck him on the hand as he was
galloping across the flats at one end of town. The sheriff
fled, and did not appear again in Mason until next day,
when he rode in with a posse of seventy-five to start a
hunt for the slayers.

This affair out of the way both sides now went out
for blood. The sheriff and the Germans took shot after
shot at the cattlemen, and the latter replied with equally
as much lead. More men were called from their homes
and shot to death . . . on both sides of the dispute.

In all this Scott Cooley undoubtedly had a hand, but
he had reserved for himself one of the most spectacular
killings of the war.

Deputy Sheriff Worley had been helping a neighbor,
Dr. Harkett, dig a well, and together they had pushed
the project down to about eighteen or twenty feet. In a
few days now, if the fine weather held out, the job
should be completed.

Dr. Harkett was working in the well, spading out
the clay and filling buckets while Worley, operating a
windlass at the top, brought the debris to the surface.
Dr. Harkett had just completed the task of setting
dynamite and lighting the fuse, and Worley had him
more than half way to the top of the shaft when Scott
Cooley appeared in the yard.

"Howdy, Worley," said Cooley, who had slipped up
unnoticed. "Guess you know what I'm here for?"

The deputy dropped the handle of the windlass and
whirled about, leaving the doctor to fall with a thud
to the bottom of the well, where the charge of dyna-

mite was scheduled to explode . . . but luckily for Harkett it proved a dud.

Worley saw in a flash that Cooley had a Winchester in his hands.

"You didn't give Tim a chance, did you?" said Scott, in the cool, hard voice which went so well with his personality. "Well, I'm not giving you one."

He raised the Winchester and fired—seven times!

Worley dropped in his tracks—and Cooley, laying aside his rifle, walked over to the well, drew a knife from his pocket, and took the dead man's scalp and ears!

These grim souvenirs he waved to all and sundry as he loped through the streets of Mason a short time later shouting in a loud voice:

"Here's revenge for Tim Williamson!"

Scott later made it clear that he believed Worley shot Tim's horse to prevent his escape that day from the posse. After the shooting of the deputy, however, Cooley made at once for the open spaces, for he knew it wouldn't be long before the Rangers would take his trail.

Captain Roberts had spent much time arguing with leaders on both sides and was making progress in his efforts to bring about peace, but now a new group of Rangers had arrived—Major John B. Jones, commander-in-chief, with his personal escort of forty men under command of Lieutenant Ira Long.

The Major gave orders for the capture of Scott Cooley, but the little officer hadn't been long in Mason before he made a startling and nettling discovery. He learned that late at night, in the shadows beyond the glare of his own campfires, some of the men of his command were receiving a visitor—and that that visitor was none other than Cooley himself!

This may seem a rather extraordinary state of affairs, but it must be remembered that in those days service with "the gentlemen in the white hats" created a traditional camaraderie and a hard-forged bond of fellowship seldom broken . . . and so it was in the case of Scott Cooley. Even some of Captain Roberts men in Company D already had resigned on the excuse that they had enlisted to fight Indians, not white men.

Cooley had served in Company D. He had helped the lads chase Comanches across the plains, and it was only natural that he should seek out old messmates. It was only natural, too, that the Rangers should sympathize and fraternize with him. As a friendly gesture Scott already had given Worley's ears to one of his old friends that the man might have some unusual souvenir of the war.

Major Jones understood all this, of course, but at the same time the Major was a stern disciplinarian and a conscientious commander, and he immediately called a parade. He told the assembled company what he had learned and how it had shocked him, and then:

"If there is any man in this outfit who doesn't want to go out after Scott Cooley," he said, "let that man step out and receive a discharge."

He waited . . . and fifteen stepped out.

But even while all this was occurring Peter Barder was assassinated as he traveled a country road in Llano county. Barder was reputed to have been present with Clark at the death of Mose Beard and his assassination immediately was coupled with the affair.

Several men took part in the killing and one of them was recognized by Lawrence Miller, who happened to be riding with Barder at the time. Thus George Gladden, though perhaps he didn't fire the fatal shot, was arrested as one of the slayers. The Rangers caught him, jailed him, and then went on Cooley's trail.

The shakeup in the state force had its effect, and thereafter Scott was seen no more about the camps. He knew now that he didn't have the moral support in the ranks. That day marked the breaking of the feud. The participants on the Cooley side, seeing that the Rangers meant business, scattered, some never to be heard from again. The citizens of Mason were not molested by the law—the general attitude being that scores were about even on both sides.

The case against John Ringgold for the Chaney slaying was dismissed, but Gladden went to trial in Llano for the Barder killing. The jury gave him a 99-year sentence, but after serving a short while he was pardoned.

According to the late Frank Moody of Fort Worth, a resident of the county at the time and a neutral spectator in the war, Captain Dan Roberts helped Sheriff Clark make his departure safely from the county . . . and the sheriff never came back.

As for Cooley the Avenger—he went to Blanco county, his former home, where he was successfully shielded by friends until his death a few years later from a cerebal hemorrhage.

—They called it brain fever in those days.

Chapter Fifteen

THE JAYBIRDS AND THE WOODPECKERS

Politics, in the traditional process of making strange bed-fellows, sometimes isn't so particular where she leaves her human puppets lie. Once upon a time down in Fort Bend county she dangled her strings and dropped her marionettes into the jaws of death, but instead of politics she called it feud. . .

In the early days of the year 1888 a meeting was held by the citizens in and about Richmond, the county seat town on the Brazos river thirty-three miles west of Houston. It was to be an important affair, and when the roll was called the sponsors were gratified to find that virtually all the more prominent planters and business men of the district, the men who really paid the bulk of the county taxes, were present.

Over on one side of the room sat H. H. Frost, J. H. Davis, J. A. Gibson, P. E. Pearson and W. D. Fields, all leaders in the social and civic life of the southeast Texas community; while across the table was ranged an equally important group which included John M. Moore, S. J. Winton and J. M. Shamblin, the latter a well-known planter on the Brazos.

The purpose of the gathering, formation of a young men's Democratic club, seemed innocent enough, but there was something deeper hidden behind the outward aspects of the situation—a seething sentiment of racial

161

prejudice and hatred which, in the end, was destined to make of that day's session the nucleus for a grim and bloody chapter in county history.

But for a moment let us look briefly at the background of the case. The trouble really had its start as a result of the Civil War. In this country of cotton plantations the negro population outnumbered the white more than two to one, and during the Reconstruction period the few white "carpet baggers" who had moved into the Richmond community had seized upon this condition as an opportunity to take control of county affairs.

The negroes, in appreciation for a new found freedom, which in addition to throwing off the shackles of slavery had given them the right to vote, were only too pleased to cast their ballots under the direction of the carpet baggers, who put up every year a full-strength Republican ticket. Thus a comparatively small faction among the whites retained absolute control of the county government, running things as they pleased and spending county money as they saw fit.

The Democrats, or the white majority, paid the bill, but not without a muttered echo of that old cry which had its origin in the early days of America's struggle for liberty—"taxation without representation." And that's about what it amounted to, this impasse in the Texas county of Fort Bend.

But now that the election of 1888 was fast approaching the long-suffering majority sought remedial measures. It was evident that something had to be done. It was bad enough that a native born Texan couldn't hold office in his own county; it was worse that the tax money he paid should be spent under the direction of a few gentlemen from the North . . . for in 1888 the various issues and hatreds of the War Between the States had not yet been forgotten.

The Young Men's Democratic Association, after preliminary organization that day in Richmond, decided that the best plan of attack would be a campaign among the negroes themselves, a campaign designed to draw enough votes from the Republican minority to sweep southern party candidates into office. No other logical plan presenting itself, committees and individuals were named to carry on the work and the meeting was adjourned subject to call—but not without two hundred names having been entered on the association roll.

The Republicans, of course, heard the details scarcely before the session was over. They met immediately, formed an organization of their own, called it the Cleveland and Thurman Club, and made plans for a counter-campaign—but they could muster only fifty members, one-fourth as many as the opposition.

It was J. M. Shamblin who made the first move. Being a large cotton planter and having to some extent the confidence of the negroes who worked his fields, he hit upon a scheme for organizing a Democratic club among the colored folk. In this he was fairly successful. Finding the negroes susceptible to his arguments for better government, he won converts to the cause, and then—

One night as Shamblin sat in the big house at the plantation reading the Bible to his family a shotgun roared outside. The charge of buckshot shattered a front window of the home and Shamblin, an unfinished line from Psalms upon his lips, toppled forward from his chair, the Bible still clutched in his hands.

The murder of the planter aroused the community, and within an hour after the tragic news reached Richmond a posse, comprised largely of Democrats, was on its way to the scene. Bloodhounds bayed that night through the Brazos river bottoms and a fresh trail, picked up in the yard of the Shamblin plantation, led to the shack of a negro field hand.

The horsemen arrested this man, who called himself Caldwell, and took him to Richmond and locked him in the jail. And then, as each Democratic leader returned home in the dawn, he found pinned to his gate or door a little note which carried this direct and simple message:

"Take warning, make no more attempts to get negro votes."

These threats, however, failed to serve the purpose for which they were intended. Rather, they raised the Democratic rage to higher pitch, and the party leaders demanded speedy trial for Caldwell, who was granted a change in venue owing to the political situation developing in Fort Bend. The negro faced a jury in Harris county where, after a brief trial he was sentenced to death and hanged.

The victory won, the Democrats then redoubled their zeal in seeking out the negro votes. They went into the shanty homes and into the fields, and in the course of time it became plainly apparent that they were making marked headway. It even appeared possible that with the election only a few weeks away the indignant tax-payers might pick up enough new votes to sweep the Republicans from power. The opposition, they reasoned, wouldn't dare resort to violence now—but the opposition did.

It happened one fine moonlit night while H. H. Frost, the Democratic leader, was out for a stroll. He walked, perhaps, for an hour and then returned home, but even as he was entering his own front gate—even as he was slipping the latch—a dark figure arose from a weed patch across the street, leveled down with a double-barreled shotgun, and pulled both triggers.

One charge of shot zipped past the intended victim's head and tore into the side of the residence, but the other caught him squarely in the back. Frost crumpled in the gateway. The assassin fled.

Attracted by the firing, neighbors rushed to the scene. They carried the seriously wounded man into his home, summoned a doctor, and then got out the hounds.

Once more the posse formed to take the trail, and again the baying dogs led to a negro shanty, but this time two suspects instead of one were brought back to Richmond jail—two negroes who might have been strung to a tree without ceremony had it not been for the doctor's report that Frost had a fighting chance to live. This good news served to allay the anger of the citizenry for the moment and the negroes were put under heavy guard to await a change in the wounded man's condition—and by the time it became certain

that Frost was on the way to recovery the mob spirit
had simmered out.

It was at this time that some of the townspeople,
most of them identified with the Democratic faction,
realized that matters had about reached the breaking
point and that some truce would be necessary if worse
bloodshed was to be avoided. Hence a mass meeting
was called, with all the whites in the county, regardless
of political faith, urged to attend.

Now the white Republicans had denied any connection with the two shootings and this denial, together
with the fact that both crimes actually had been perpetrated by negroes, served to draw the party factions
a bit closer together, at least in racial harmony. Thus
it was that when the mass meeting was called to order
Republicans and Democrats sat down side by side to
thresh out the community problem.

First action was in the form of a resolution stipulat-
ing that certain negroes, known trouble-makers, must
depart from the county, and in this both factions
agreed. Then the Republicans sprang the great surprise.

In order to safeguard the peace of the county at a
critical period in its affairs, said the Republicans, they
had decided for once not to nominate a ticket for the
coming election! They would make Fort Bend county
safe for democracy!

The Democrats, of course, were speechless with
amazement, but they managed to swallow their surprise
and launch plans for a full ticket of their own . . . not
neglecting to dispatch a message to Major Haywood
Brahan, prominent state party leader, asking him to

visit Richmond and help celebrate the joyous occasion.

In due time the major arrived and another mass meeting was called—this time to name the county ticket. With harmony the keynote everything went off with the utmost decorum. The candidates for the various county places were selected and nominated. The steamroller was oiled, and things looked rosy for the Democratic party . . . too rosy, in fact, as subsequent events were to prove.

The ink on the new ticket was scarcely dry before a certain element in the Republican faction became obsessed with the idea that the Grand Old Party, through its local leaders, had been over-hasty in withdrawing from the field; and the more they considered the matter the more difficult it became for them to drop peacefully out of the picture.

Accordingly, their small group—knowing that they could have the negro vote for the asking—proceeded to put out a ticket of its own. They called themselves Independents, or Conservative Democrats. And here the matter stood—the old-line Democrats against the "Conservatives."

Naturally, animosities flamed again and a hot campaign ensued. The negroes listened as both sides grew eloquent in argument.

"A bunch of Jaybirds!" sneered the former Republicans, referring to the old-liners.

"A gang of Woodpeckers!" replied the Democrats, as they went from one plantation to another decrying the infidelity of their opponents.

And thus originated the title which the two factions

were to carry, and take pride in, through all the tur-
bulent months to follow. The names, though first offered in derision, caught on even though the parties did
label each other, and it wasn't long before the Republican was going about calling himself a Woodpecker,
while the Democrat stressed the fact that he was a Jaybird—"and proud of it."

And then, after various street brawls and fist fights,
election day arrived, and when the last vote was counted
it was discovered that local history again had repeated
itself. The so-called Conservatives, with the help of the
negro votes, still held the county courthouse.

During the weeks immediately following the election
feeling ran higher than ever in Fort Bend county.
Neighbor passed neighbor on the street without speaking, relative argued with relative, but the first actual
bloodshed to result from the situation occurred not in
Richmond, but in two other towns, and in two different
counties.

L. E. Gibson had been the Jaybird candidate for
county assessor in opposition to Kyle Terry of the
Woodpeckers, and through a peculiar turn of fate the
two chanced to visit the city of Wharton on the same
day. They met, and hot words passed . . . and when the
smoke had cleared away Gibson the Jaybird lay dead
in the street.

But retribution wasn't long in overtaking the Woodpecker. A week later Terry and Volney Gibson, a
relative of the deceased, happened to be visiting in
Galveston on the same day, and they chanced to meet
on the steps of the county courthouse. Gibson drew his

gun and fired . . . Terry sagged to the steps and died.

—And the proverbial calm before the storm settled over the streets of Richmond as Volney Gibson came home under bond. The town, tense with expectancy, waited—for they knew not what. One thing seemed indicated . . . more bloodshed . . . and men went about armed against that day.

The hope of peace now appeared too remote for serious consideration. Too many men had been killed— first Shamblin, then Gibson and Terry, to say nothing of Frost's near fatal wound. Only the spark was needed to set the flame. Months passed, and then, on August 16, 1889, that spark was struck . . . by Albert George, who even from the first had cast his lot with the cause of the Jaybirds.

There are those who say that George merely feigned a disturbance, that his conduct in the streets of Richmond was only the part of a pre-conceived plan to bring long-smouldering issues to a head, but whatever the case Mr. George surely started something.

He had scarcely been taken in tow by the Woodpecker sheriff of the county, J. T. Garvey, than Vol Gibson stepped into the streets with a Winchester rifle in his hands.

Over in front of the courthouse were three Woodpeckers, Deputy Sheriffs Tom Smith and H. S. Mason, and J. W. Parker, a former county judge; and as Smith and Mason saw the approach of the sheriff with a prisoner they went to meet him. Judge Parker, recognizing the man as a Jaybird and seeing Gibson in the street, sensed trouble. He drew his pistol. Gibson raised his

Winchester. The battle of Richmond was on . . . a roaring skirmish in the sunset.

The slayer of Kyle Terry had pumped no more than a couple of empty cartridges from his rifle before the street was filled with a motley swarm of both Jaybirds and Woodpeckers, all armed and eager to join the fray.

Heavy Colt revolvers began to roar from all points along the block facing the courthouse entrance . . . and the melee, steadily becoming more general, was punctured by the whanging crack of Winchesters brought into action by belated participants.

J. W. Blakely, a former sheriff, was the first to fall. Stepping from a store at the outset of the battle, he died on the sidewalk, a rifle bullet through his body.

Sheriff Garvey, whose prisoner had fled at the first burst of gunfire, went down next. With his two deputies he had tried to reach the safety of the courthouse but on the lawn . . . within a few yards of the door . . . he fell, virtually riddled with bullets.

Deputies Smith and Mason dropped down beside him and prepared to return the Jaybird fire, but even as they raised their pistols Mason was put out of action by a hunk of lead which tore a gaping hole in his left shoulder.

Darkness had now set in, but Smith, aiming across the unlighted street, emptied his own revolver and then those of Sheriff Garvey and Deputy Mason at targets which were little more than shadows moving across the building fronts. Spurts of fire flashed from a dozen points, but Smith escaped unhurt. One of the Jaybird bullets, however, did catch Private Jones of the Texas

Rangers, who came out of the courthouse with Ranger Alex McNabb to carry back the sheriff.

The two state officers, who had been in the courthouse when the battle started, advised Deputy Smith to get under cover, but he refused to leave until Garvey's body had been removed and Mason had been carried to safety. He wasn't scratched but when he reached the courthouse he found Ranger Jones with a bullet through one thigh, and Judge Parker lying on a cot in the courthouse, a rifle wound in the groin.

The judge had fallen by the door of the building and the Rangers had previously carried him inside.

With the withdrawal of the sheriff's party the firing stopped, but it was not until daybreak that the full extent of casualties became known. The score stood:

Jaybirds—Three wounded, one fatally.

Woodpeckers—Two dead and one wounded.

Non-combatants—One dead, a negro girl hit by a stray bullet; one wounded, the Ranger.

The mortally wounded Jaybird was H. H. Frost, the Democratic leader and organizer. Even with his shotgun wounds not entirely healed, he had entered the scrap at the start. He had stopped four bullets which, within a few days, were to prove fatal.

Volney Gibson and W. M. Andrus were the other wounded Jays. Andrus had been shot in the calf of one leg, and though the blow had knocked him down, he stayed on the square until the fight was over.

A rifle bullet had given Volney Gibson a back collar-button. The ball had entered his jaw, passed through the neck, and had stopped to form a lump at the back of the neck. But he had kept his feet during the fight, and in the morning, after eating a hearty and leisurely breakfast, went to the doctor and had it cut out.

The post-mortem on the sheriff revealed that he had borne the brunt of the fight for the Woodpeckers, for Garvey had received one bullet through the heart, three in the abdomen, two in the right leg, and one in the left. In addition a hole had been cut by a slug through the crown of his hat.

Long before daylight the telegraph wires were carrying urgent messages to Governor Sul Ross at Austin. Ross immediately ordered troops to the scene—twenty-four officers and men of the Houston Light Guard under Captain F. A. Reichardt, and forty men and officers of the Brenham Light Guard under Captain J. M. Byrnes.

They arrived to find the town quiet, but they arrested twenty-five men, all of whom later were released.

Governor Ross, a former Ranger and Indian fighter, visited the town himself, and while there made the suggestion that Ranger Sergeant N. A. Aten be made sheriff to replace Garvey. He believed that with a neutral man in that office much trouble might be avoided in the future. The Jaybirds thought the plan a good one, but it was several weeks before the Woodpecker commissioners court would fall in line and make the appointment.

After that peace reigned in Fort Bend county. One by one during the next few weeks the Woodpecker office holders began resigning and one by one the Woodpecker families began moving from the county.

Even while the exodus was under way the old line Democrats called another mass meeting for the announced purpose of "combining and uniting the white people for the advancement and prosperity of the county."

The meeting was held October 3, 1889, and out of it came an organization which was to take great pride in its name—the Jaybird Democratic Association. They wrote a constitution that day and in it they included this clause:

"We therefore declare that any white man, now residing in this county, who shall undertake to lead against this association any political faction or voting population opposed to the principles and objects of this association, shall be considered and treated as a social and political outcast."

Then they erected a monument to the three Jaybirds who lost their lives in the conflict—Shamblin, Gibson and Frost.

Is there any need to add that Republican votes, even today, are scarce in Fort Bend county?

INDEX

Colt revolver, 78
Cooley, Scott, 152, 156, 159
Cox, William, 88, 95
Cravens, Col. James F., 33, 40, 41, 42, 44, 45
Cuero, Texas, 73, 74, 77, 79, 88

Daggett, Eph M., 13, 14, 17, 18, 21, 27, 39, 41, 43
Daggett, Helen Mar, 27
Daniels, J. M., 129, 131
Davis, Gov. E. J., 131, 132
Davis, J. H., 161
Denson, Sheriff S.T., 133
Denton, John B., 54
De Soto Parish, Louisiana, 24
De Witt County, 67, 68, 73, 74, 77, 80, 82, 87, 92, 93, 95
Dispatch (Lampasas), 130

Ellis, Charles E., 111, 113-115, 119
El Paso County, 113
El Paso, Texas, 107, 117, 125

Farrar, John, 35, 36
Fields, W. D., 161
Fort Bend County, 161-173
Fort Davis, Texas, 102
Fort Stockton, Texas, 102
Fort Worth, Texas, 13
Franklin, Texas, 112, 113
Frost, H. H., 161, 165, 171

Galveston, Texas, 168
Gandara, Madonia, 109
Garcia, G. D., 116, 119, 120
Garcia, Gregoria N., 108
Garcia, Miguel, 116, 119, 120

Garvey, J. T., 169, 170, 172
George, Albert, 169
George, Hezekiah, 56
Georgetown, Texas, 133
Gibson, J. A., 161
Gibson, L. E., 168
Gibson, Volney, 168, 169, 171
Gill, James, 52
Gillette, J. T., 90
Gladden, John, 152, 153, 155, 159
Gonzales County, 68, 74
Goodbread, Joseph, 11-16
Grafton, William, 83
Granillo, Leon, 109, 113-115
Gross, August, 98
Guadalupe Mountains, 107

Haley, Thomas, 40
Hall, James, 33
Hall, Joseph, 31, 32
Hall, Lt. Lee, 87-80, 91-94
Hall, Samuel, 29
Hardin, John Wesley, 69
Harkett, Dr., 156
Harrison County, 44, 51, 53, 58
Hays, Black Matt, 15
Heissig, Charles H., 88, 95
Helms, Jack, 69
Hendricks, ____, 80, 81
Henry, Tyler, 61
Hester, James, 88, 95
Higgins, J. Tom, 146
Higgins, John H., 134
Higgins, John P. C. "Pink" (photo), 128, 134-139, 143-145
Hillard's Spring, 44, 45
Hoerster, Daniel, 154, 155